ETHICS
AND
SPIRITUAL CARE

ETHICS AND SPIRITUAL CARE

A Guide for Pastors, Chaplains, and Spiritual Directors

Karen Lebacqz
Joseph D. Driskill

ABINGDON PRESS
Nashville

ETHICS AND SPIRITUAL CARE:
A GUIDE FOR PASTORS, CHAPLAINS, AND SPIRITUAL DIRECTORS

Library of Congress Cataloging-in-Publication Data

Lebacqz, Karen, 1945-
    Ethics and spiritual care : a guide for pastors and spiritual directors / Karen Lebacqz, Joseph D.Driskill.
        p. cm.
    Includes bibliographical references and index.
    ISBN 0-687-07156-9 (alk. paper)
    1. Pastoral theology. 2. Clergy—Professional ethics. 3. Spiritual directors—Professional ethics. I. Driskill, Joseph D. II. Title.

BV4011.5 .L42 2000
241'.641—dc21

00-032287

00 01 02 03 04 05 06 07 08 09—10 9 8 7 6 5 4 3 2 1

14399

CONTENTS

ACKNOWLEDGMENTS

W e would like to thank the faculty, administration, support staff, and students of Pacific School of Religion for the variety of ways in which they supported our research interests through probing questions, engaging conversations, attention to detail, and the oftprovided inquiry, "How is the book coming along?"

We thank those groups of persons for whom one or both of us led workshops where the topic of spiritual abuse was discussed: Presbyterian clergy gathered at the Mercy Center, Disciples gathered for the Disciples Seminary Foundation annual Berkeley lecture, lay leaders from groups in Southern California and Oregon.

Last, we thank our families and friends for their understanding and support. Lara Cross, Joe's niece, enjoyed generating names for use in the case studies, and Leslie Bryant generously read and suggested valuable amendments for selected sections.

INTRODUCTION

We need an expert witness," the caller said. I groaned inwardly. Since the publication of *Sex in the Parish*, my life had been too full of cases involving allegations of pastoral sexual abuse. I started to decline, but then stopped as my caller explained her agenda. The charges, she said, were not of sexual abuse but of *spiritual abuse.*

This was a new term to me. With trepidation, I agreed to appear as a witness in this church proceeding. I began searching the literature to find anything I could that would help to clarify the boundaries and meaning of this new term. I consulted with my colleague Joe Driskill, who teaches spirituality at Pacific School of Religion. Both of us were troubled by the phrase "spiritual abuse." We feared that "abuse" was once again being bandied about in vague and unhelpful ways. Our discontent led us to ask what would constitute *good* spiritual care. We began to organize a series of workshops, which we carried out over the next several years. This book is the result of those workshops, and we are grateful to all who helped us in our struggles to come to terms with an elusive term that threatens to become the basis for a new wave of clergy misconduct allegations.

Our purpose here is not to settle the question of whether there is such a thing as spiritual abuse. Nor will we be able to define its boundaries with exactitude. Our agenda is both more and less ambitious. It is more ambitious because we want to address the broader questions: What constitutes good spiritual care? When it comes to caring for the "spirits" of the people they work with, what are the basic ethical obligations of spiritual directors, parish clergy, and those in specialized ministries? How do we know when those obligations are fulfilled? Is there a difference between spiritual abuse and simple incompetence or neglect? If so, what is that difference?

At the same time, our agenda is less ambitious. We intend to begin here a "mapping" project: mapping what we have come to call a muddy terrain. Our purpose is not to provide definitive answers, but only to show how complex the questions are, and to find some footpaths that others might follow as they, too, struggle to navigate the territory. At the end of this book, there will be no checklist to show when behavior is right or wrong. There will probably be as many questions as there were at the outset. But we hope that there will be some moments of clarity and some guideposts to assist the courageous traveler down the road.

Some Quandries

Consider the following scenario, for example. Helen is nineteen and wants to join a religious group that has very strict rules. If she joins, she will have to change her name. She will not be allowed to speak unless directed to do so by a superior. She will have to give up all her possessions, wear the distinctive garb adopted by the group, and leave her home to live at group headquarters. The religious group will become her new "family." They will determine where she lives, what she eats, what she does every minute of her day. She will not be allowed any sexual activity, nor will she be able to use a telephone or initiate contact with her family of origin. She will spend at least four hours a day in prayer, much of it on her knees. She will be expected to fast at least one day a week. She may be required to engage in ritual chanting.

Helen's mother is not happy about this. She worries that her daughter, young and impressionable, has been "brainwashed" by the group. She thinks maybe her daughter is a victim of spiritual abuse. She begins to consult with authorities about what her rights are if her daughter decides to join this group. She reads up on cults. She consults her local minister.

If you were that minister, what would you say? Do the requirements of this religious group constitute spiritual abuse? Helen's mother thinks so, but Helen does not. Many mainline Protestant ministers would probably think so. Images of "Moonies" and other cults come to mind. But what if we told you that the scenario just described is not that of a prototypical cult, but is in fact that of entry into some Roman Catholic religious orders? While it is many parents' nightmare that their child might join a cult, it is equally many parents' dream that their child might become a nun. Can equivalent strictures be acceptable spiritual discipline when required by a prominent, well-established church, and spiritual abuse when required by a relatively unknown and more marginalized sect? This is troubling. It shows us that we tend to label something "spiritual abuse" when we do not like it or when we associate it with something that is not accepted mainstream practice. But liking or not liking something does not automatically make it right or wrong, and being mainstream also does not justify religious practices. Many practices that we would probably consider abusive today were once accepted practice in most Protestant as well as Roman Catholic churches. Fasting, long hours of prayer, ascetic practices involving sexual deprivation or plain clothing—these are all part and parcel of the history of mainstream practices in numerous denominations.

Let's take another scenario. Central Baptist Church—a predominantly African American church in a large metropolitan area—has just lost its beloved pastor of many years. Hezekiah Jones was loved by the congregation because of his mesmerizing preaching and his kind and pastoral presence. He often visited members of this aging church, and always had his shingle out for them to drop by and talk. His retirement is a blow to many longtime members. When Albert Woodman is called to the church, he finds an elderly congregation. He also sees an opportunity to do social justice ministry. He starts a neighborhood watch program to reduce drug abuse in the area; he begins a coffeehouse to get kids off the streets; he joins an interfaith soup kitchen effort. His community activities keep him so busy that he has little time for pastoral calling, though he knows that deacons follow up when there is illness or special need in the church. Church programs are thriving, but some longtime members begin to complain because their pastor is not easily accessible.

Is Albert Woodman practicing good spiritual care by pushing Central Baptist into the local community? Or is he neglecting the spiritual care of parishioners who used to depend on their private time with the minister? Recent studies suggest that congregations that do not adapt to the changes happening in their neighborhoods will die.[1] Is it appropriate to focus on such adaptation, even when it creates dissent and makes congregants uncomfortable? Is it appropriate to keep doing things the way they have always been done, at the risk that the church will die? Which approach constitutes good—or bad—spiritual care in the midst of changing circumstances? Does ethical spiritual care involve meeting the needs of parishioners as they perceive those needs? Or does it mean getting behind their perceived needs or desires to something more basic? Who should determine what constitutes good spiritual care?

A third scenario involves the rising interest in "spirituality" today. Many people who are not associated with any particular denomination or church consider themselves very spiritual. They engage in a wide variety of practices, often drawn rather eclectically from different religious traditions. They may do yoga as a daily form of meditation, keep a journal as yet another spiritual discipline, and attend a wicca ceremony monthly. In chronicling her own spiritual journey, for example, Winifred Gallagher notes that she spent considerable time learning Zen meditation and was deeply moved and uplifted by the experiential liturgy of B'nai

12

Jeshurun, a Conservative Jewish synagogue in New York, before finally turning to the Episcopal Church to find a church home.[2] As church members become interested in the gifts that different religious traditions bring to spiritual growth, pastors will be pressed to stretch their own understanding of acceptable practices. Suppose Donna asks her pastor to join a yoga practice group in the church. At the same time, Christine has gotten very interested in Buddhist meditation, and wants the pastor to initiate a Buddhist meditation session for parishioners. Ted has been reading Robert Bly, and decides that his spirituality will be fostered by founding or joining a group to chant and beat drums in a male ritual adapted from Native American spiritual practices. Should pastors support such efforts? Join them? Initiate them? Critique them? If so, under what conditions? Is it acceptable to adopt the practices without studying or believing in the underlying religious worldviews? Is it disrespectful to other religious groups to adopt some of their practices out of context? What kinds of spiritual practices should clergy encourage?

Here is yet another scenario. Suppose you are a denominational official in Basic Mainline Denomination. Insurance for your denomination is carried by Church Life, Inc. In the last several years, Church Life has received a number of complaints about clergy, including the allegations of spiritual abuse with which we opened this introduction. As a result, Church Life is growing leery of clergy who claim to do spiritual direction. They are afraid that they are going to incur a series of suits against clergy based on claims of spiritual abuse; after several large settlements for sexual abuse, they consider Basic Mainline Denomination a potential liability. Church Life declares that it will no longer carry insurance for Basic Mainline Denomination unless the denomination establishes standards for spiritual direction, and ensures that only those clergy who meet the standards are in fact practicing spiritual direction.

What should those standards for spiritual direction be? Is

it realistic to assign such standards in a mainline denomination? How would denominations ensure that only clergy trained in special ways do spiritual direction? Would that mean that other clergy are not providing spiritual care? What distinction should be made between the spiritual care given by parish pastors and the "spiritual direction" to be provided by those who are specially trained? Don't *all* clergy provide spiritual direction in some sense? How are churches to sort out such distinctions and put them into practice?

These are only a few of the scenarios with which we have struggled. Others will be introduced later in the book. What is good spiritual care? How is it affected by the context of ministry? What are the ethical issues that arise in providing spiritual care? How are these issues affected in turn by ordination and various ministerial contexts? Such questions provide grist for our mill.

The Game Plan

We begin in Part I by making an effort to map the muddy terrain. Here, we encounter two immediate problems. First, "spirituality" is a slippery and indefinite term. Although it is in wide use today, definitions of spirituality are almost as numerous as the people who use the term. When two people consider themselves "spiritual" or speak of their "spirituality," it is not clear that they mean the same thing. Second, "ethics" is also a slippery and indefinite term. Although there is a lot of talk about ethics today, almost no one agrees on what is meant. When two people consider themselves "ethical" or speak of something as "unethical," it is not clear that they mean the same thing. Is it possible to have ethical standards in a pluralistic world? Moreover, there are controversies today over whether clergy can simply adopt the standards of professional ethics that apply to other professions. What should be the grounds and the content of clergy ethics? The indefiniteness of both of our key terms—"spirituality" and "ethics"—creates immediate problems for defining ethics in the arena of spiritual care. Our effort here is to sort out enough of the confusion so that we can proceed in Part II to some of the specific ways in which a ministry of spiritual care is practiced: spiritual direction, parish ministry, and specialized ministries such as chaplaincy or teaching. In this section, we will explore in more depth some of the particular dilemmas that clergy face when giving spiritual care in different contexts.

Finally, in Part III we turn explicitly to the question of spiritual abuse. We review the literature on this topic, raise some questions and challenges to the use of the term, and make an effort to distinguish abuse from mere incompetence. Although we will highlight different forms of unethical practice of spiritual care, our overall purpose is to offer guidelines that assist clergy in providing good and even excellent care.

It is our conviction that clergy have one of the most demanding and difficult jobs in the world. It is also our conviction that spiritual care is of the essence of ministry in all its various settings, and that clarity about what constitutes good spiritual care is crucial for clergy, for the church, and for the well-being of all God's people. We hope that this little volume opens a dialogue to enable better spiritual care and more appreciation both of its demands and of its centrality in our lives.

PART ONE

MAPPING
A MUDDY TERRAIN

CHAPTER 1

The Many Faces of Spirituality

Everywhere we turn today, "spirituality" is in vogue. Cultural cachet is obtained for many pedestrian topics simply by attaching to them the word *spirituality*. Even practices of rest or relaxation in the workplace are called "spiritual" enrichment. Both pop culture and academic treatises cash in on the popularity of this term.

But what is spirituality? If clergy are to provide good spiritual care, they must first know what constitutes the "spiritual" dimension of life. Immediately, we encounter a problem: although "spirituality" seems at first a simple and obvious term, on deeper reflection it becomes more than a little complex and can even be obscure. Consider the following pair of comments about spirituality:

> "I have nothing to do with organized religion, but I'm very spiritual."[1]

> "The spiritual is the deepest sense of belonging and participation."[2]

The first comment assumes that it is possible to be "spiritual" without an organized religion, the second that spirituality and a sense of community go together. What is the role of "belonging and participation" in fostering spiritual growth? Can one be spiritual on one's own? Without religion? Can one have it both ways?

Consider another pairing:

> "Spirituality is otherworldly."[3]

> "To separate spirituality from the rest of life . . . runs against the very nature of spirituality."[4]

Is spirituality otherworldly? Can it be separated from "the rest of life," from material things? Is it true spirituality if it is? Can one have it both ways?

Finally, consider the following comments:

> "To heal the spirit involves creating a pathway to sensing wholeness, depth, mystery, purpose, and peace."[5]

> "Christian spirituality is about a process of formation . . . in which . . . we are transformed so that we come more and more to share the Christ nature."[6]

Does spirituality have to do with taking on a "Christ nature" or simply with sensing wholeness, purpose, and peace? Are they the same thing? Is there a distinctive Christian spirituality? If so, what are its marks? Can one have it both ways?

As these quotations show, there is no single agreed definition of *spirituality*. The diversity of groups interpreting spirituality creates some of the confusion: some consider it the province of Christianity or of religion more broadly, while others think it has to do with what is most deeply human and need not be connected to religion at all. Some refer to historically accepted practices or definitions, others to whatever they have found most useful or healing. Speaking ironically, noted Episcopal lay leader and ethicist William Stringfellow once declared:

> "Spirituality" may indicate stoic attitudes, occult phe-
> nomena, the practice of so-called mind control, yoga
> discipline, . . . an appreciation of Eastern religions, mul-
> tifarious pious exercises, . . . intensive journals, dynamic
> muscle tension, assorted dietary regimens, meditation,
> jogging, cults, monastic rigors, mortification of the flesh,
> wilderness sojourns, political resistance, contemplation,
> abstinence, hospitality, a vocation of poverty, non-
> violence, silence, the efforts of prayer . . . or, I suppose . . .
> squatting on top of a pillar.[7]

If everything from political resistance to yoga to "squatting
on top of a pillar" can be considered spirituality by some-
body, is there any point to using the term at all? Can we
make sense out of this cacophony?

We think so. True, we face here a "muddy" terrain. So
many feet have tramped about in the waters that the
riverbed has been stirred up and it is now difficult to see
with clarity the beautiful rocks below. It is hard to know
where to step. Yet we believe that there are stepping-stones,
and that they can be pointed out, so that the intrepid traveler can begin the journey across the waters. In this chapter
we will survey some definitions and approaches that we
hope will lay out focal elements necessary for understanding
spirituality in the contemporary setting. We will also note
some of the ethical questions that emerge as each set of focal
elements becomes clearer. These questions will help to frame
our later discussion.

Spirit and Spirituality

The root of spirituality is spirit. The *Oxford English
Dictionary* offers some twenty-three definitions of *spirit* as a
noun, and eight as a verb. Some of these contribute little to
the topic at hand—for instance, those concerning distilled
spirits!—but others suggest that two foci must be held in creative tension.

21

The first focus is the human spirit—the notion of a life force that animates human beings:

> a) The animating or vital principle in [a person] . . . which gives life to the physical organism, in contrast to its purely material elements; the breath of life; b) a particular character, disposition, or temper existing in, pervading, or animating a person. . . ; a special attitude or bent of mind . . . ; c) the essential character, nature, or qualities of something; that which constitutes the pervading or tempering principle of anything.[8]

Note that these definitions speak not only of something that "animates" humans, but also of that which gives us our distinctive character or essence. Thus, "spirit" means something that is central and essential to who we are as human beings. Note that these definitions also give some nod to the idea that "spirit" is to be contrasted to "matter"; this gives force to the popular notion quoted above that "spirituality" has nothing to do with our "material" selves. We will return to this again.

The second focus is the divine spirit, which in Christian tradition is the Spirit of God or Holy Spirit. Definitions here include:

> a) the active essence or essential power of the Deity . . . ; b) the Holy Spirit; c) the active or essential principle or power of some emotion, frame of mind, etc., that operates on or in persons.[9]

These definitions point to Spirit as an essence and as a power of the divine that may be active in human life.

Approaches to spirituality will differ in their understanding of the human spirit, the divine spirit, and the relationship between them. These differences bring some ethical concerns: Is divine spirit, for example, primarily a loving and forgiving presence in human life, or is divine spirit a judging and condemning force? Does the divine spirit work in the human arena, and if so, how? Are Wisdom and Sophia—both understood as feminine principles—appropriate interpretations of Spirit? Is human spirit created in the image of divine spirit? Is human spirit good or corrupted or incomplete?

A crucial divide is whether one understands "spirituality" to be something that humans possess independently of the working of a divine spirit. The first "stepping-stone," then, in our muddy terrain, is recognition of the importance of clarifying what role, if any, the divine spirit is playing in people's understandings of spirituality. Since this book is primarily geared to those in the Christian tradition, most of our readers will not make such a separation. But it is important to remember that the term "spirituality" as it is used today increasingly connotes a stance that may separate humans from any sense of the divine or of the workings of a Holy Spirit in people's lives. Too much emphasis on Spirit will not connect with many people's understanding of their spirituality; too little emphasis on Spirit runs the risk of pandering to modern temperament at cost to the integrity of Christian tradition.

Three Approaches to Spirituality

As the next stepping-stone, we propose Bernard McGinn's threefold division of definitions of *spirituality*.[10] One tends to separate spirituality from divine spirit; two incorporate an understanding of the divine, but in different ways.

1. Anthropological Definitions

McGinn calls definitions of *spirituality* "anthropological" when they focus exclusively or primarily on *human* spirit. Here, spirituality is seen as an element in human nature, frequently a depth-dimension of human existence. This approach considers "spirituality" to consist in human authenticity, self-transcendence, and the experiential dimension of human existence. The approach is reflected in the first set of definitions of *spirit* from the dictionary.

23

Even Christian theorists sometimes work with anthropological definitions. Noted scholar Sandra Schneiders says spirituality concerns "the experience of consciously striving to integrate one's life in terms not of isolation and self-absorption but of self-transcendence toward the ultimate value one perceives."[11] This definition speaks of "ultimate value" rather than of God. It leaves open the possibility that one might be spiritual without relating specifically to a Godhead.

A similar definition is given by Ronald K. Bullis: "Spirituality is defined here as the relationship of the human person to something or someone who transcends themselves."[12] Bullis makes clear that this broad definition "is intended to include the enormous variety of transcendent values, concepts, or persons with which people identify as higher sources."[13] Either religious or secular language and concepts would be compatible with such a definition. Spirituality understood this way might explore the personal biography of a figure or group, for example, to determine what inspired someone to "greatness" or leadership. The approach seeks to find the "spirits" that guide human lives beneath the surface. By starting with human experience, rather than with faith affirmations or traditional doctrine, such approaches allow a wide berth for understanding spirituality.

2. Theological Definitions

For some, the anthropological definitions allow *too* wide a berth. Terms such as "depth" of human existence are too vague. They do not help to clarify what is inside the purview of spirituality and what is outside. Indeed, they appear to give rise to precisely the array of activities that William Stringfellow so derisively lists.

For some, true spirituality happens only when human spirit and divine spirit are connected. Theological definitions therefore tend to stress the divine spirit. They begin with the assumptions of a particular faith tradition. For example, Walter Principe defines *Christian spirituality* as "life in the Spirit as brothers and sisters of Jesus Christ and daughters and sons of the Father."[14] In such a definition, there is no "spirituality" without "Spirit"—human and divine spirits must be connected. Here, spirituality is understood by one's relationship to a community of faith, be it Christian or Jewish or other.

Such definitions help faith communities to situate themselves, but may not help them to address those outside the tradition. It is sobering to remember that "seven in ten Americans believe that one can be religious without going to church" and that "in the new millennium, there will be a growing gap between personal spirituality and religious institutions."[15] Christian groups who insist on theological definitions may find themselves not speaking to the majority of spiritually inclined "neo-agnostics," to use Winifred Gallagher's term.[16]

3. Historical-Contextual Definitions

Principe's definition speaks from a broad understanding of the community of faith, trying to encompass all Christians at once. However, it is possible that particular traditions (Lutheran, Roman Catholic, Calvinist) would have even more refined understandings of appropriate spirituality. Historical-contextual definitions are rooted in a particular community's history and experience. Here the rituals, values, beliefs, and attitudes of the community—its particular animating "spirit," if you will—give definition and meaning to the practice of faith. For example, Hinson suggests that both Baptists and Quakers differed from Catholics in their stress on individual rather than corporate spirituality, yet differed from each other in their styles of worship and prayer, among other things.[17] The black church tradition in the United States sees spirituality as having a distinctive connection to the struggle for social justice.[18] As Bernard McGinn himself puts it,

25

spirituality here is "the effort to appropriate Christ's saving work in our lives." It stresses "those acts in which the relation to God is immediate and explicit."[19] Historical-contextual definitions recognize that we are socially located and that this social location gives meaning and purpose to human life. It shapes what we perceive and what we do. When Sandra Schneiders turns to an explicitly Christian understanding of spirituality, for instance, she defines *spirituality* as "the conscious striving for self-integration toward the God who is revealed in Jesus and is present as Spirit in and through the community of faith, the church."[20] In such a definition, there could be no genuine spirituality apart from participation in a distinctive community.

This definition does not presume that all human spirituality is the same, therefore. For instance, women claiming their own modes of spirituality might resist anthropological definitions, even as they use some of the language that anthropological definitions provide. But women are seeking an understanding of spirituality that is distinctive to the context of *women* and that takes seriously women's historical struggle for liberation. Reflecting on the possibilities for women in the church, one woman said, "I think it's all hopeless. We must dump Christianity and start over—or go back to the Goddess."[21] A definition of *spirituality* based on such a community's history and experience might include the necessity of relating not to God or to the Holy Spirit, but to Goddess or to Wisdom-Sophia.

These three approaches—the anthropological, theological, and historical-contextual—are not necessarily incompatible. Although each characterizes an emphasis in approaching spirituality, elements from all three may be present in each. What this stepping-stone allows us to do is to ask whether we have attended adequately to all three dimensions: to the importance of that which is ultimately and distinctively *human,* to the role of *theology* or the *divine,* and to the particular *historical* and *contextual* situation in which our spirituality must find expression. For example, we would argue that post-Holocaust Christian and Jewish spiritualities must attend to the significance of this event as an expression of extreme evil in the world. If our expressions of spirituality cannot confront such evil and denounce it, then they are not adequate expressions of spirituality. We will return to this question in chapter 4 when we look at charges of spiritual neglect.

Devotional Literature and Spiritual Growth

A great deal of the current literature on spirituality is geared toward the edification of the believer or practitioner. Books on "enhancing your spiritual growth" abound. Some of these focus on the spiritual growth of the individual within the framework of a religious tradition. Others distinguish spirituality from religion, often debunking religion as they support nonreligious approaches to spirituality. Our third stepping-stone consists in evaluating the approach taken by such texts.

Within religious traditions, books on spirituality often focus on personal spiritual growth. They advocate practices such as prayer and devotional reading. In both Protestant and Catholic circles, devotional magazines encourage readers to develop and deepen their relationship with God (e.g., *Alive Now, Upper Room, Praying, Spiritual Life, Weavings*). Articles often detail stories of faith, offer poems dealing with important life transitions understood from within a faith paradigm, and provide introductions to spiritual practices—for example, the role of silence in prayer or an explanation of the labyrinth as a spiritual exercise. Most of these books are concerned with prayer and contemplative practice. Few, for example, urge political involvement as a mode of spirituality, though historically such involvement has been quite important in Christian spirituality. (Think, for example, of the nonviolent disciplines engaged in by African American Christians during the Civil Rights struggle.)

In *Taste and See: A Personal Guide to the Spiritual Life,*

William Paulsell describes the nature of religion in terms of an experiential relationship with God: "Religion is our personal relationship with God. That is the essence of it."[22] Paulsell contends that our social action and service, and even our church life and morality, "are religious only if they are grounded in our experience with God." His introduction to the spiritual life is useful, and shares with many other resources a focus on developing an experiential relationship with God. The primary focus is helping the individual become more faithful by establishing, nurturing, and maintaining a personal relationship with the divine. Yet this emphasis on *personal* relationship would not stand the test of some definitions of *spirituality*, and it may reflect more the modern American setting than it does a historical appreciation of Christian faith.

A slightly different emphasis is offered by Kenneth Leech. At first glance, Leech's definition appears similar to Paulsell's, in that Leech stresses spirituality as a process of formation: "a process in which we are formed by, and in, Christ."[23] However, Leech is quick to point out that being incorporated into the body of Christ involves incorporation into a community where social context is a constituent element in living a faithful life.[24] People by their very nature are participants in political and economic communities. These wider communities also stand under the judgment of God's will and activity. Leech therefore provides a vision of spirituality that sees transformation in Christ not simply as an individual transformation, but as a call to see all of life as an arena for spiritual development. Here spirituality is not disconnected from the material world, but intimately yoked to it. This becomes important, as we will see in discussing the four components of an adequate "grid" for spirituality.

Supported by the individualism of the surrounding culture, many contemporary devotional approaches encourage a relationship with God that pays scant attention to matters of justice within the wider community. Some contend that religion has little to do with politics. Yet the current agendas of the religious right as well as the traditional social involvement of mainline denominations encourage an understanding of spirituality that links it to the political arena. Individual morality or faithfulness that neglects larger justice concerns is an oxymoron—it simply is not possible for those who would be true to Christian faith and community.

Michael Downey addresses both the personal-experiential and the community-justice aspects of Christian spirituality. Christian spirituality "refers most fundamentally to living the Christian life in and through the presence and power of the Holy Spirit."[25] It involves the quest for the integration of mind, body, and soul. For the Christian this spirituality is rooted in the mystery of the Trinity where community rather than individuality is emphasized.

> The goal of the spiritual life entails perfection of one's relationships with others, rather than an ever more pure gaze of the mind's eye on some eternal truth "out there" or in one's interior life. From this perspective, spirituality naturally connects with the ethical demands of the Christian life, which flourishes in the increase of communion among persons. . . .[26]

Downey's understanding of Christian spirituality places it within the wider frame of "the human quest for personal integration in the light of levels of reality not immediately apparent."[27] For the Christian this quest for integration is focused not on self-absorption or isolation, but on relationship with God, Jesus Christ, and the Holy Spirit.

Spirituality Versus Religion

However, not all the literature derives from or addresses Christian community. A growing body of resources maintains a sharp divide between spirituality and religion. According to Wade Clark Roof, most baby boomers (born between 1946 and 1964) make a distinction between spirituality and religion. They characterize spirituality as subjective, personal, and potentially enriching for the faithful practitioner. Religion, by contrast, is viewed as an external, institutional, and objective religious expression. "To be religious conveys an institutional connotation: to attend worship services, to say Mass, to light Hanukkah candles. To be spiritual, in contrast, is more personal and empowering and has to do with the deepest motivations of life."[28] We have already noted that seven out of ten Americans think it is possible to be religious without going to church. Although church memberships have been declining, belief in prayer and other spiritual practices remains strong: 87 percent of Americans believe that God answers prayers and 85 percent say they continue to pray even when they feel their prayers are unanswered.[29] Thus, Americans clearly separate church and institutional religion from prayer and spirituality. While shunning formal practices of religion, many Americans are "seekers"—searching for personal meaning, including personal relationship with God. Thus, they have a keen interest in spirituality, understanding it as something that is possible apart from religious community or institution.

This overwhelming interest in spirituality, and the separation of it from formal and traditional religious institutions, is given expression in a number of ways. New Age spiritualities, Eastern religious practices, 12-step programs, Wicca groups, or Sophia circles—these and many others provide avenues for spiritual development for people who feel estranged from institutional religions.[30] The pluralism represented by such groups is now an acknowledged aspect of daily life. In the contemporary context, we will inevitably come face-to-face with people pursuing forms of spiritual practice that differ from our own practices. Living in the midst of such diversity raises a number of ethical issues: On what grounds do we adjudicate between spiritual claims? What does it mean to maintain the integrity of a particular religious stance? Are we free to use Eastern practices in Western contexts without adopting or even understanding their original context? When do religious or spiritual practices become destructive or abusive? Is there an ethics of mutual respect that should be incorporated into spiritual practices? If so, what is it?

These concerns are a helpful reminder of the necessity of humility in Christian tradition. Perhaps it is salutary for us that we are no longer dominant in the culture, and that we must learn to live peacefully with people whose spiritual practices are so different from ours. But for pastors and other spiritual leaders, the pluralism of our world is also troubling. This emphasis on personal spirituality, and the tendency to divorce it from religious tradition or community life, is particularly troubling from a Christian perspective.

Guidelines for an Adequate Christian Spirituality

In the midst of such secular pressures to separate spirituality and religion, it may be presumptuous to suggest that there are guidelines for an adequate Christian approach to spirituality. What we suggest here is very minimal, but we think it may be helpful for clergy and other Christians seeking ethical avenues to spiritual growth and nurture.

1. Spirit and Spirit

Christian spirituality must hold in tension the stress on Spirit as well as spirit. Approaches to spirituality that stress *only* the growth of human spirit are not fully Christian. In Christian tradition, our spirits are not fulfilled until they "rest in God." We seek "perfection" in the sense of an ever-closer relationship to the divine. This is sometimes expressed in the phrase "imitation of Christ," though the term "imitation" needs some nuancing. Those giving spiritual guidance in Christian tradition will want to bring people closer to God and will understand that fullness of human spirit depends on such a relation between spirit and Spirit.

31

2. Discipline

In *Celebrating Disciplines,* Richard Foster, a Quaker, commends the use of spiritual disciplines, not with the aim of obeying an externally imposed "proper religious practice," but because such disciplines are an aid to spiritual growth. Driskill has noted in his earlier work that there are two main paths to spiritual growth: although some people experience life-changing spiritual events at times of crisis, most people are helped by undertaking spiritual exercises in a disciplined manner.[31] Such disciplines "help those who long after God to become deep people who commit the whole of their lives to the transforming work of the Spirit of Christ," claim Foster and Yanni.[32] The point here is that true Christian spirituality takes discipline. It will not necessarily come easily, nor feel comfortable.

3. Accountability

Maria Harris provides a definition of *spirituality* that integrates a response to the sacred with ethical behavior: "I use the term *spirituality* to refer to our way of being in the world in the light of the Mystery at the core of the universe; a mystery that some of us call God." Harris continues: "The term also requires understanding what the Mystery requires of us, such as the classic set of demands recorded in Micah 6:8: 'to do justice, and to love kindness, and to walk humbly with your God.'"[33] Here we see demonstrated the need to be accountable to the work of God as it is understood within the boundaries of a community of faith. The focus is not simply on the Spirit as it is present in the lives of individual believers, but on a sense of accountability to the Scripture text within an established canon. Similarly, Foster lifts up not only *internal* disciplines such as prayer, fasting, or meditation, but also *outward* disciplines such as service and living simply, and *corporate* disciplines such as worship, confession, and spiritual guidance. True Christian spirituality does require what Bonhoeffer once called "life together" in order to ensure accountability to text, tradition, and community. True Christian spirituality will involve community, and it will involve accountability structures.

4. The "Grid"

The theological assumption that underlies Christian spirituality is that God is at work in our lives. Within such a framework, however, we may tend—as our culture is clearly inclined to do—to look only for God's activity in the arena of *personal* life. A corrective to this highly individualistic approach is found in a scheme Jack Mostyn calls the "grid."[34] The "grid" is composed of four elements: (1) the *intra*personal, (2) the *inter*personal, (3) the *structural,* and (4) the *environmental* aspects of life. Using the grid, persons seeking spiritual growth must look not only at their own intrapersonal issues and relationship with God, but also at the ways in which God may be at work in social relationships, the institutions and structures of the wider society (including but not limited to the church), and in the environment as a whole. Using the grid requires that attention to the inner life of search be placed in the context of concerns about social, historical, environmental, structural, institutional, and interpersonal issues. We propose that a Christian approach to spirituality must attend to all four elements of the grid.

Even so, ethical questions may arise. For instance, growing numbers of people inquire about the everyday ramifications of their beliefs, including the role of spirituality in the workplace. Some writers, such as Mary Anne Williamson, focus on such matters as "smiling more" or "whistling more" as a spiritual practice to make the workplace a happier and more productive environment. Some employees are requesting appropriate space for lunchtime prayer groups and Bible study.[35] Although we applaud attention to the work environment as a context for spirituality, this does not remove ethical concerns: Is it moral to improve my personal spiritual life without considering the implications of the company's behavior overall, both for its immediate community and for the environment? Does the "product" of this company have implications for the spiritual well-being of consumers both here and abroad? Is it ethically problematic to use spiritual disciplines to improve workplace productivity rather than as an expression of faithfulness to God? Does making the workplace more humane ever clash with standards for integrity? These are some of the questions that might emerge in a dialogue between spirituality and ethics.

The guidelines we offer here are very minimal and do not provide a full "path" through the muddy terrain. However, they do suggest a direction and some stones on which we can step in the midst of muddy waters. They tell us that spiritual care in a Christian context connects human spirits with the divine Spirit. They tell us that spiritual care in a Christian context will require discipline and possibly hard work. It will not necessarily come easily, nor will it always "feel good" to adherents. Spiritual growth can come from struggle and pain as well as from experiences of joy and lightness of being. The guidelines tell us that spiritual care in a Christian context will require a community and a system of accountability to God, text, and tradition. Finally, they tell us that spiritual care in a Christian context demands a focus not merely on our "inner state of being" but on relationships, structures, and even the entire environment.

This is a tall order. The task of the spiritual care giver is to facilitate the discernment of the Spirit and its movement in our lives. This sounds simple, but in a world filled with difficult ethical dilemmas, it is often not easy to discern the leading of the Spirit or its meaning for us. Should we abandon traditional language of Holy Spirit, for example, in favor of the language of "Wisdom" or "Sophia"? How do we remain faithful to tradition, while not shutting out the ongoing movement of the Spirit in Christian community? To whom are we accountable as we attempt to discern where the Spirit blows?

The first ethical task of the spiritual care giver may well be the choice of an understanding of spirituality and of an approach to spiritual care. Without a clear understanding of what lies inside appropriate spiritual direction and growth, and what lies outside, it is impossible to give care to those in one's charge. What if someone is relating to "goddess" instead of "God"? Is this acceptable? Am I focusing on the human spirit or the divine Spirit? Is my definition broad enough to allow me to reach those whose backgrounds differ from mine? Is it narrow enough to be responsible to God and the church? For what purpose and in what contexts do I use the term "spirituality"? How accountable am I—if at all— to a community of faith? These very difficult issues suggest that clergy and other spiritual care providers cannot simply plunge into giving care, but must be reflective about the meaning and limits of what they do and even of how they define the crucial terms.

In the next chapter, we attend to some definitions and understandings of ministry and its ethical requirements. These definitions and understandings will also establish a rudimentary framework for the ethical provision of spiritual care.

CHAPTER 2

Ethics for Clergy

Just as approaches to spirituality abound, so do approaches to ethics. Several decades ago, ethics was largely understood as a matter of rules and principles. Today, commentators stress character and virtue[1] or liberation from oppressive ideologies and structures[2] or seeking the right ends.[3] The field of ethics offers little clarity when we try to find a base for clergy ethics.

Worse yet, the last two decades have seen a spate of books on clergy ethics, arguing for different starting points. Many earlier books, including Lebacqz's *Professional Ethics: Power and Paradox,*[4] took note of the fact that ministry is a classic profession and therefore assumed that models of professional ethics drawn from other professions such as medicine were applicable to the plight of the pastor. Early books in this field often took for granted that broad analyses of professional ethics might be helpful to clergy, and that clergy ethics was really a variant of professional ethics generally.[5]

Recently, however, the use of a professional ethics model

for clergy has come under attack from within the theological community:

- from those who say the model doesn't fit *ministry;*
- from those who say it doesn't fit *women* in ministry;
- from those who say it doesn't fit *new* or *developing* ministries;
- from those who say the *model itself* is bankrupt, for ministry and other fields.

The crucial issues raised by these critiques cause us to look again at the relationship between the professional model and the ethics of spiritual care.

What is the professional ethics model and what is the controversy about? Is the professional ethics model useful at all for those in ministry? Will it help us develop an ethical framework for spiritual care? What models best fit our understanding of ministry today, as faces and contexts change, and what are the implications of different models for the provision of spiritual care? This chapter makes an attempt to answer these questions by listening to multiple voices to see if any clarity or commonality can be found and to discern what it might mean for the ethics of spiritual care. We begin by looking at the professional model itself.

The Professional Model

There is no single agreed definition of what makes a profession. Nonetheless, a growing consensus in recent years does locate some key features and their implications for professional ethics. In a recent essay, Camenisch identifies four distinguishing marks of a profession:

1. *Specialized skills and knowledge,* acquired by extensive education and resting on a theoretical base;
2. *Professional autonomy,* not simply in the sense of a great deal of freedom in how one practices the profession, but in

the sense that only one's peers can assess the value of one's work, that the profession itself can expel members who are not up to expectations, and that the profession controls entry into professional practice;

3. *A distinctive goal* (such as health or spiritual well-being) that is valued by society; and

4. *Motivation outside personal gain*—particularly, an atypical moral commitment to the interests of clients.[6]

Camenisch suggests that power, status, and income are derivative rather than constitutive of being professional; however, others suggest that professionals are characterized precisely by the *power* that they have over their clients.[7]

The Power Differential

Although Camenisch does not identify the imbalance of power between a professional and a client as a distinguishing mark of a profession, much recent work has focused on professional power and its serious implications for the development of professional ethics. The power gap between professional and client is understood to be morally relevant: it places obligations on the one *with* power to avoid harming the less powerful and to do good *for* the client. Thus, we might say that from the traditional model of professional ethics that stresses the skill, knowledge, autonomy, service orientation, and unselfish motivations of professionals, comes an understanding of professional ethics characterized by:

- Recognizing the power gap between professional and client: professionals have power, where clients are vulnerable;
- Understanding that those with power are responsible for behaving appropriately—for instance, for setting appropriate boundaries;
- Accepting fundamental norms of "nonmaleficence" ("do no harm") and "beneficence" ("do good"). These norms

reflect the understanding that those with power over the vulnerable are to avoid harming their clients and to work for the client's good over their own good.

Thus, professionals are often understood as having a *fiduciary* relationship with the client, based on the power differential. This fiduciary relationship obligates professionals to work for the good of their clients, and not to harm them. Professionals are not supposed to be motivated by their own gain, but rather by what they can do to serve client needs. They are expected to uphold the highest standards of *trustworthiness,* such as keeping confidence.[8] The practice of a profession thus becomes linked to notions of service, trustworthiness, and non-exploitation. This is why we are so outraged at stories of psychiatrists or ministers who abuse their patients or parishioners sexually: they violate every accepted norm of professional behavior when they exploit clients and seek their own interests rather than meeting the needs of the clients they are to serve.

With this characterization in mind, it is easy to understand why ministry is often understood as a profession. Clergy "profess" something. They profess a faith in God and an adherence to the traditions of the church. They have special skill and knowledge at communicating those traditions. They are supposed to put their own needs aside (even to the point of working at poverty wages) in order to serve their congregations. Finally, they are under strict obligations of trustworthiness that include stringent conditions, such as the "seal of the confessional," which prohibits clergy from divulging confidences. As Marie Fortune summarizes, the pastoral relation is one of unequal power, and unequal power requires a fiduciary responsibility to act in the best interests of the congregant.[9]

Clergy Ethics and the Professional Model

In spite of these similarities to classic understandings of professions, there have always been voices arguing that ministry is not a profession or cautioning that the professional ethics model does not fit ministry well.[10] Today, there is a growing consensus that "clergy ethics" needs its own terms and justifications, and cannot simply be subsumed under professional ethics more broadly.

The reasons for this uneasiness about classical definitions are many. First, clergy do not seem to fit exactly the four chief criteria of a profession (skill, autonomy, goal, and motivation) outlined by Camenisch:

1. Although clergy have specialized skill and knowledge, they are not always required to have extensive education, nor are there clear and universally defined standards for what their skill and knowledge should be. Rather, expectations of training and skill differ from denomination to denomination, group to group. Further, clergy skills are not as consistently valued by society as are skills of other professions such as medicine.

2. Many clergy have considerable autonomy over their work. Yet they are not insulated from lay judgment to the extent most professionals are. Clergy are not licensed by the larger society, nor does the profession as a whole admit them into practice; rather, they are admitted by specific denominational bodies that may have widely varying standards. In some denominations, for example, one cannot be ordained without a "call" from a local church, whereas in others ordination is not contingent upon a local call. Where laypeople serve as "gatekeepers" into a profession, they have considerable power over the professional. Thus, it may not be professional peers alone who determine one's standing in ministry.

3. There does not appear to be agreement on the goal that is served by this "profession"—is it salvation of souls? faith? the increase of the love of God? the maintenance of the church and its ministry? social justice? Although one could probably say that clergy have a central role in

dealing with "spiritual" dimensions of life, the meaning of this goal and its implications for ministry would not necessarily be agreed upon among denominations or groups.

4. Finally, the "service" rendered is not necessarily rendered to an individual client such as a patient. Indeed, it may not be rendered to human clientele at all, but to God. The understanding of a transcendent realm within which the meaning of ministry takes shape makes this "profession" distinctly different from others.

In light of this review, Camenisch concludes that it is not sufficient simply to define a profession and then to see whether clergy fit the definition. Both the imprecision of "profession" and how the role of clergy is variously understood work to defeat any simple correlation. There are enough similarities between clergy and other professions to appropriately deem the clergy a profession, but enough differences that clergy cannot be entirely subsumed under the professional model.

Indeed, Camenisch suggests that clergy may carry the *burdens* of other professionals—for example, the commitment to client well-being—without reaping the *benefits* accorded other professional groups—for example, autonomy. He notes that the commitment to serving the interests of the client may be so strong in ministry that this emphasis has actually prevented the development of specific ethical standards that protect professionals in other settings. Finally, he suggests that there are dimensions of the clergy's calling that derive *not* from their skill and knowledge, but from "the transcendent source of their ultimate authority as religious leaders."[11] Hence, professional ethics may set a floor below which clergy should not go, but an additional source of ethics is needed— a "higher" ethic that will sometimes demand that clergy forsake the rewards of professionals and even stand over against society. Finally, Camenisch notes that professional power may be itself a temptation, a seduction against which clergy should be constantly on guard.[12]

The Call to Lead a Community of Faith

Others point out that the professional model tends to be based on an assumption that professionals deal one-on-one with clients, whereas clergy deal with a *community* of faith, an *institution*—the church.[13] "Equipping the saints" for the work of ministry[14] is done not just one-by-one, but in the context of the "body of Christ." The better pastor, suggests Donna Schaper, "prepares the congregation."[15] That is, while other professionals such as doctors or lawyers may deal with individual clients, clergy usually deal with an organized clientele. This structural difference is significant.

Many see the responsibility for leading a community of faith through the theological notion of "calling," and not simply as "a job." This calling of clergy—to the ministry of Word and sacrament—is formally recognized by the faith community through the act of ordination. Yet at the time of the Protestant Reformation Martin Luther and John Calvin both rejected notions that elevated religious vocations above those of others who saw their work as service to God. H. Richard Niebuhr notes that the call to be a Christian comes to all believers.[16] Thus, the theological nature of calling would not in itself put clergy beyond the pale of professional standards when other occupations may also be understood theologically as callings.

Walter Wiest and Elwyn Smith propose a model for clergy ethics that recognizes the institutional nature of the ministerial calling. They call their model the "watching brief."[17] Recognizing that different denominations understand ministry differently, Wiest and Smith nonetheless suggest that there is considerable agreement about the meaning of ministry. That agreement centers on the concept of *service*. The model of service is based on Christian affirmations of what it means to call Jesus the Christ. Thus, any authority in ministry must be consistent with the demands of service. Ministry is required of all Christians, yet some are "set apart" through ordination. Wiest and Smith propose that the special responsibility of those who are set apart is "watching" over the purity of the church's proclamation, understanding proclamation to include both word and deed. In other words, "the pastor has a special . . . responsibility to see that the congregation stays on track, to be sure that what it does is consistent with the gospel and is fitting for the body of Christ taking shape in the world."[18] In other words, all Christians "proclaim" the word by what they do and say, but the task of the clergy is to step in whenever this proclaimed word would be brought into disrepute.

Such an understanding brings with it a clear mandate for clergy to exercise authority by correcting the congregation. If Albert Woodman believes that his church has neglected social justice issues, and that this imperils its proclamation of the word, he would be doing good spiritual care in "correcting" them, in this view. Although correction will no doubt raise questions about the meaning and practice of spiritual care (see chapter 6), what is crucial for our purposes at this point is to note that the clergy, in this view, relate primarily to an institution and have a primary responsibility for monitoring the shape and character of that institution. This differs from the traditional model of professional ethics that focuses on the relationship between two people, one of whom is the professional and the other the client.

Of course, any distinctiveness of clergy in this regard depends on *context.* Some clergy do indeed serve in a parish where ministry to a congregation is their primary responsibility, and where they may deal with organized groups of parishioners more than they deal with individuals. But other clergy serve in chaplaincies, or in ministries of spiritual direction or pastoral care where their primary "clients" may indeed be individual parishioners or patients or persons seeking a particular skill, and where dealing with groups or organized clientele may be an occasional rather than regular responsibility. Moreover, any number of other professionals also serve in institutional settings with some primary responsibility to an organization rather than simply to individuals within it: engineers may serve a university, physicians may be hired by corporations, and so on. There are difficult questions of potential conflicts in such settings, since the good of the institution and the good of the individuals within it may not always coincide. Such conflicts may also characterize clergy who serve in parish or institutional settings. The fact of having an organized clientele, rather than operating one-on-one in the paradigm of some traditional models of professional ethics, does not distinguish clergy alone, but is becoming more and more prevalent in professional ethics generally. Thus, this characteristic is important to remember for clergy but does not necessarily mean that models of ethics developed for other professions are inapplicable.

The Role of Denominational Context

Nonetheless, the church may be a distinctive sort of institution. Pushed to its logical conclusion, the view that clergy ethics must be seen in light of the church might even suggest that clergy ethics is *determined by* the institution.[19] Gilkey proposes that different denominational traditions have different ecclesiologies, and that these shape attitudes, expectations, and practices. In Gilkey's view, ecclesiological convictions set the tone for expectations and obligations of the clergy. For example, in a *sacramental* church the minister serves as sacramental mediator. Here, the personality of the clergy may be far less important than the preservation of traditions and rituals that convey the sacramental power embodied in the church. Performance of the eucharist may be the key function of clergy and may be seen as central to spiritual care. In a *church of the word,* by contrast, tradition and ritual may be less important than the power of the pulpit, and preaching rather than eucharist may become the central act of the church and hence of the clergy.

Such an understanding has implications for the ethics of spiritual care. In a sacramental church, for example, spiritual care might be understood to center in the performance of the sacraments. Failures of care might be judged by how many congregants do not receive the sacraments, or how many fail to request "last rites" or other sacramental interventions. In a church of the word, by contrast, good spiritual care might be understood to rest not in the performance of sacraments but in providing challenging and compelling sermons that inspire the laity or lead people into an experience of God's presence. In one denomination, failure to visit the sick might be understood as the most egregious breach of professional ethics and subject the minister to severe reprimand, whereas in another denomination the same failure might be greeted with a puzzled shrug of the shoulders. Defining the boundaries of professional ethics would therefore need to be accomplished denomination by denomination, group by group (and in some cases, church by church). In this case, it would be difficult to offer any suggestions for clergy ethics across the board.

Rebecca Chopp, addressing primarily mainline Protestant denominations, contends that church must be a "constitutive community of emancipatory transformation." As a result of her theological commitments she calls the professional model "the best and worst model" for clergy ethics. It is "best" because it *can* offer standards of excellence. But it is at the same time "worst" because it "threatens to suffocate ministry with bureaucratic rationality and technical service."[20]

Chopp's "constitutive community" is a community that forms our identity and shapes our ethical commitments. To be a Christian is to be formed and shaped by membership in a community with a common history and a shared set of convictions. To be a Christian is to see the world in a particular way, and to live out of certain values.[21] We do not simply "join" a church but are "constituted" by our membership in it.

By "emancipatory transformation," Chopp intends to lift up the metanoia that is supposed to characterize Christian life. Not just *any* change will constitute emancipatory transformation, however; only change geared toward liberation will be understood as emancipatory. Hence, in Chopp's view, the church is called to be a "visible sign of grace" that models liberation in the world. The minister, then, is not a *professional* who professes, organizes, keeps the institution running, and upholds tradition, but is an *artist* who stirs people's imaginations, a *community builder* who enables congregational identity, a *prophet* who critiques dominant and nonliberating practices in the culture, and a *teacher* who equips people to name their world and to think, dream, and sing God's praises. In a twist on the old saying that Christians are to be "in but not of" the world, Chopp proposes instead that Christians are to be "in but not of" the church, for it is the church itself as institution that most needs emancipatory transformation. If clergy are to provide that transformation, they cannot operate out of traditional "professional" models.

These voices and perspectives suggest some profound challenges to the professional ethics model. Not only do clergy serve an institution as well as individual clients, and not only are expectations of clergy shaped by understandings of church, but the institution that they serve is dedicated to certain values that may not be well served by maintaining traditional models of professionalism—or even of church! One way or another, all of these commentators suggest that traditional models of professional ethics may have merit in themselves, but are not necessarily applicable to clergy, because of the distinctive setting, role, and calling of the ministry.

Gender, Ethnicity, and Sexual Orientation

While some see the professional model as not applicable to ministry in general, others think it has a place, but a limited place. Clergy themselves are changing, as any seminary can attest. The faces of those entering our seminaries look very different today from the faces we saw twenty years ago. What happens when clergy are women? Or when they are gay men serving gay communities? Or when they are Hispanic, Asian American, or Native American men and women? Does the traditional model of professional ethics fit these alternative groups? Some would say No.

In *Leading Women: How Church Women Can Avoid Leadership Traps and Negotiate the Gender Maze,*[22] Carol Becker argues that women bring different leadership styles into ministry than do men, thereby understanding the ministerial role differently than men do. To the extent that traditional professional ethics is derived from and geared toward the role understandings of men, therefore, such traditional ethics simply do not apply to women. Women tend to be *process* rather than *outcome* oriented, suggests Becker. They use a participatory style of management. They show little interest in being the "expert" and are fundamentally oriented toward maintaining relationship. Their style tends to be informal, open, and intimate. Since the traditional model is based on understandings of an appropriate *distance* between professional and client, it does not fit well with the *intimacy* that women bring. Thus, the traditional model of professionalism might be appropriate for *male* clergy but might not fit well the many *women* who are going into ministry.

Above all, the traditional model of professional ethics, as noted, assumes that there is a power gap between professional and client, and that this power gap is morally relevant. But is there a power gap when the professional is a woman? Becker argues that women respond to power ambivalently. They tend to eschew power, seeing it as selfish and not helpful to ministry. Moreover, it is not clear that women *have* or *could* have power in ministry, even if they wanted it. Becker documents the phenomenon of the "invisible woman" whose ideas are credited to others and who is discredited if she attempts to claim authority. Thus, to the extent that the traditional model of professional ethics is based on the assumption that there is a power gap between professional and client, and that this power gap brings responsibilities to the professional, it is not clear that women have this power or the responsibilities that are assumed to go with it.

Stories of clergy women tend to confirm some of these differences noted by Becker. Some women in ministry deliberately develop what they consider a feminist style of leadership that is collaborative and nonhierarchical.[23] Others call their leadership style "leading by following," with an emphasis on lay leadership in the church.[24] Donna Schaper suggests that instead of professional *skill*, what is needed in ministry is care.[25] The gifts and graces of care, she notes, come not from professional training but are formed in and by community. Similarly, in *Co-Creating: A Feminist Vision of Ministry*, Lynn Rhodes argued for friendship as a model for ministry, in contrast to traditional arguments that clergy should not be friends with their parishioners.[26] Speaking out of her Hispanic context, Mari Castellanos notes that in the Hispanic community, parishioners expect their pastor to be a friend, not a "professional" with all the distance that this term implies.[27] For all these women, then, the traditional professional model is problematic because it accepts uncritically the power of professionals, assumes that leaders are formed by training and education rather than by community, and implicitly adopts a hierarchical model of relationship.

Notions of professional power imply hierarchical modes of relationship that are specifically rejected by many women and members of minority communities. To the extent that professional ethics is based on assuming such power gaps, the professional model may not fit the realities of nonpowerful people going into ministry, and may also not be appropriate to the nature of the institution served.

Boundary Issues: Gender and Cultural Implications

This brings us to the most radical objection: that the professional ethics model itself is bankrupt. This objection holds that not only does the professional ethics model not fit the people who are going into ministry today, but it never should have been used for *anyone* going into ministry, because it is based on assumptions that reflect a dominant culture that oppresses rather than liberates.

We have stated this view strongly here, but not much more strongly than it is stated by some of the most ardent critics of the professional model. The publication of Carter Heyward's *When Boundaries Betray Us: Beyond Illusions of What Is Ethical in Therapy and Life* set off a storm of controversy over models of professional ethics.[28] Using her own experience with a therapist, Heyward argues *against* traditional understandings of the appropriate boundaries between therapist and client. Specifically, she argues that therapists *can* and sometimes *should* be friends with their clients. While she never says outright that a sexual relationship would also be acceptable, she borders on removing all of the traditional "boundaries" that have characterized a long struggle to clarify appropriate relationships between professionals and their individual clients. The concept of boundaries, suggests Heyward, is used uncritically today. "This absolutizing of boundaries serves to reinforce the abusive logic upon which the healing professions have been structured in the first place—that is, to hold patriarchal power in place."[29] It is no wonder the book was instantly very controversial and problematic!

In a later reflection, Heyward, together with her longtime colleague and friend Beverly Harrison, argues explicitly that the notion of "boundaries" itself is destructive of professional practice.[30] To be sure, Heyward and Harrison acknowledge, we need ways of protecting against abuse, sexual and otherwise. But they challenge the notion that keeping to a strict understanding of "boundaries" is the proper way to avoid abuse. Good boundaries, they argue, are not the way to secure "right relationships." Indeed, the concept of boundaries itself comes from ego-psychology and therefore reflects the capitalist and male-dominated culture in which psychology developed.[31] The concept of "boundaries" presupposes a well-defined self that exists primarily for itself: the purpose of "boundaries" is to protect this self. "This psychology, with its adamant defense of 'self' and 'boundaries,' functions to hold existing power relations in place, not to change them."[32] In religious community, suggest Heyward and Harrison, pastoral care should embody ways of healing that constantly challenge such individualized and elitist professionalism.

Heyward and Harrison therefore explicitly challenge the notion that clergy cannot simply be peers among their congregants. They criticize denominational statements that lift up the power of clergy and see it as morally relevant. They propose that, instead of a model of clergy-congregant relations drawn from assumptions of transference and professional power, churches should be striving for relations of mutuality and friendship. To reify clergy power is simply to collude in undermining conditions of creative freedom in the church. Worse yet, they propose, codes of clergy ethics based on assumptions that clergy power must be contained have simply worked to undermine genuine ethical reflection and behavior among clergy. They therefore call for a *"communal* reconception of professional ethics in the churches."[33]

This critique is nothing short of a call for an entirely different base for clergy ethics. Like Gilkey's proposal that different ecclesiologies shape different understandings of clergy behavior, Heyward and Harrison's proposal, taken to its logical end, suggests that nothing short of communal agreement would establish the base for appropriate clergy ethics. This might leave clergy ever more dependent upon the particular community being served, and suggests that clergy ethics would be relative to each community.

Though not pushing quite so far as do Heyward and Harrison, Leng Leroy Lim gives some support to their suspicions about "boundary" language and concepts.[34] The notion of boundaries, suggests Lim, is very Western—indeed, very American. Americans have a strong assumption that they should have "private space" protected by boundaries from the intrusions of others; in East Asia, by contrast, to delineate such boundaries "is tantamount to hostility and inhospitality."[35] Further, suggests Lim, the logic of boundaries may work against us: if boundaries are understood in the language of isolation, violation, and invincibility, then we are likely to confuse safety with invincibility and therefore often to feel violated or victimized. Boundaries language reflects the underlying assumptions of autonomy, which looms large in American culture. When we confuse autonomy with freedom, we assume that we can live happily while isolated and disconnected from others. By contrast, suggests Lim, to be in the body of Christ is to believe that we are deeply connected to others. Our erotic feelings are precisely a way of experiencing that connectedness, and so Lim suggests that we do not serve the church by trying to repress and deny all erotic feelings, or place "boundaries" around them. Our mystical experiences cannot be separated from our concrete embodiedness. In somewhat Jungian fashion, Lim suggests that we must pay attention to our "shadow" sides—to those sides of ourselves that we would rather not see—or we will fail to deal with the pain in our individual and collective lives.

Yet Lim finally concludes that in order for us to explore our embodiment and face our pain, "there needs to be preparation, intentionality, the setting of limits, and the securing of boundaries."[36] Writing from both cultural and sexual margins, Lim is keenly aware of how any ethic can become life-denying to those who are different. Nonetheless, in order to allow safe exploration, he finally suggests that some limits and boundaries will be necessary. This is reminiscent of Castellanos's call for permeable boundaries that allow *some* things through, but not everything.

Toward Rapprochement?

What are we to do with this cacophany of voices? With so many different approaches and understandings of ministry and ministerial ethics, it is no wonder that some clergy are confused or feel that they are left without adequate guideposts. While some may be working hard to establish themselves as "professionals," others are working just as hard to undermine the credibility of that image! How are we to find standards of ethics in the midst of this confusion of images, ideals, and models?

All is not lost. Not all of these voices can be reconciled, but we believe that it is possible to find a path through the thicket and to come out on the other end with some assistance for clergy ethics so that we can say something about ethics and spiritual care.

First, few voices would give up completely the understanding that clergy do tend to have power over parishioners. Even Heyward and Harrison, who urge us to work toward mutuality and who reject any assumption that power attaches to the *person* of the minister in perpetuity, acknowledge that structure and culture tend to put clergy in a *position* of unequal power over clients. Heyward and Harrison find such unequal power ethically unacceptable. The task, then, is to work to undo the inequality—to strive for mutuality and friendship in the midst of structures that make it difficult. Such a view characterizes other feminists as well: the goal of mutuality is accepted, but implicit with that goal is an understanding that mutuality is *not* provided by the structures in which clergy practice.

If even the harshest critics of "boundaries" do nonetheless begin with an assumption that there tends to be unequal power between clergy and parishioner, then the relevance of the professional paradigm becomes apparent. Even if clergy do not like to be considered professionals, even if they strive for mutuality and intimacy rather than "professional distance" from their parishioners, any existing power gap—whether welcomed or not—means that ethical constraints similar to those of the traditional professional ethics model will be important. Those with structural power have a fiduciary relationship to work for the good of the less powerful. What Harrison and Heyward help us to see is that this "good" might need to be defined in terms of empowerment or mutuality, not simply in terms of beneficence or doing good for the client.

Indeed, many years ago, Karen Lebacqz suggested precisely that the power of the clergy brought with it an ethical obligation to seek the empowerment of the parishioner.[37]

However, what Lebacqz failed to do at that time was connect this understanding of the ethical obligation to seek power to its true ecclesial roots. What Wiest and Smith, Gilkey, and others[38] help us to see is that the obligation to empower the powerless derives not simply from a generalized base of "professional ethics," but from an understanding of the nature and function of church. To the extent that church is to be Chopp's "constitutive community of emancipatory transformation," to the extent that the church is to liberate the oppressed, to "bring good news" to the poor, and to lift up the lowly, then those who are given structural power within the body of Christ are ethically required to ensure that the whole body functions to do precisely that. The "watching brief" of Wiest and Smith is not antithetical to an understanding that clergy work with institutions in the interests of liberation and justice.

Yet the "watching brief" still implies a kind of professional distance. Can it be reconciled with the notions of friendship and mutuality, of permeable boundaries and intimate connectedness, that come out of the voices of women and other marginalized people? We think so, provided we understand that different ecclesiologies will indeed tend to support different understandings of the proper role and place of clergy. This is where Gilkey's insights become most helpful. How much intimacy, and how much distance, are appropriate in ministry may not be able to be settled with a single "rule" for all clergy—neither a rule of distance nor a rule of intimacy. If clergy ethics depends to some extent on ecclesiology, then what we understand "church" to be will determine to a large extent what styles and models of ministry are most fitting. As women and members of other disadvantaged groups enter ministry, the understanding of church itself wiil change. Women may "lead by following" or by encouraging others, but this in itself does not mean they have abandoned a form of "watching brief." They may simply be doing their "watching" in a different guise.

In short, we think that there are valuable insights to be

gained from all the voices raised on the topic of clergy ethics. Certainly we would concur with Heyward and Harrison that boundaries should not be reified. Clergy ethics is not simply a matter of setting appropriate boundaries, and as we explore ethics and spiritual care, this will become evident. At the same time, protections against abuse must be structured into any clergy ethics, if those ethics are to be credible. This has been true in the arena of sexual abuse, and it will be true in the arena of spiritual abuse. This, too, we will explore in what is to come. The creation of genuine community may be at the core of all good clergy ethics, and this will affect how clergy understand their role in providing spiritual care. Finally, it is important to remember that clergy are providing spiritual care in very different settings and contexts, and that these settings may also be crucial. Appropriate behavior in a parish setting may not coincide with appropriate behavior in a more specialized ministry setting. In particular, there are differences in structure between pastoral counseling and spiritual direction, and these differences become important for determining the ethical components of good spiritual care. It is to these issues that we turn in the next chapter.

PART TWO

SPIRITUAL CARE
IN CONTEXT

CHAPTER 3

Pastoral Care and Spiritual Direction

One Sunday the Reverend Dr. Sarah Lockhart, Senior Pastor of First Methodist Church, is approached after church by Alice Gartz, a forty-year-old member of the congregation and a lifelong United Methodist. Alice has a positive relationship with Sarah, and decides to speak with her about some difficult personal issues. Alice has two children: Heather, a fifteen-year-old daughter, and Matt, a ten-year-old son. Alice and her husband, Ted, attend church two or three times a month. Alice approaches her pastor with anxiety in her voice and tears in her eyes over her daughter Heather's plight. Heather's grades dropped sharply about the same time she started hanging out with a group of older kids. Alice has always had a close relationship with her daughter, but lately feels a growing distance between them. God has looked after Alice's family in the past. Now that things are not going so smoothly, Alice is worried that somehow her faith or her prayers are not acceptable to God.

Sarah readily agrees to meet with Alice for two or three hour-long sessions. By the end of the first meeting Sarah suggests to Alice that she might pursue some pastoral counseling with a pastor in the community who does longer-term pastoral and family counseling. Alice has never talked so personally with her pastor before, and she has never gone for any type of counseling. Their session leaves Alice with a powerful sense of relief. At least she has someone with whom to speak confidentially.

The following Sunday Sarah finds herself in a conversation with John Dickson, a member of First United Methodist Church. He had not planned to have an extended conversation with Sarah after church, but her sermon on prayer touched a deep place of yearning within him. In his early fifties, John had for many years taken time each day for silent prayer, a practice he learned in a church retreat a number of years before. For a few years he went to a Roman Catholic sister for spiritual direction. This had been a most helpful relationship and had helped him understand the importance of prayer for his daily life. About a year ago his spiritual director was moved by her order to another community. John intended to find another director but has not done so yet. Recently he participated in a study group exploring the spirituality of John Wesley. His interest was piqued and he realized he had not spoken in depth to anyone about his prayer life since losing his director. John knows that Sarah is interested in prayer and makes herself available to members of other congregations for spiritual direction. He is not sure why she does not see people from First Church but thinks it must have to do with boundary issues. From her sermons, like the one this morning, he knows that she understands the importance of the spiritual life. He has heard her talk at length about how she believes a pastor should be a guide or director for the congregation as a whole, so he believes she will be able to help him find someone with whom he can once again discuss his prayer life. Sarah agrees to meet with John two or three times to discuss his concerns and tells him she will be delighted to suggest some ways in which he might pursue spiritual direction.

In the cases of Alice and John we find a number of aspects of spiritual care that a pastor can provide. Although many people today in mainline Protestant communities are discovering the importance of spiritual direction, greater numbers are confused about its meaning. People who have grown up in mainline Protestant churches are accustomed to terms such as pastoral care and pastoral counseling, but spiritual direction seems to be a form of pastoral attention that is difficult to distinguish from pastoral care and counseling. In some instances the differences between these professional activities are subtle and the practices overlap. However, there are also some identifiable characteristics that differentiate pastoral counseling and spiritual direction.

In this chapter we will use Sarah's experiences to provide examples of the ministries of pastoral care, pastoral counseling, and spiritual direction. We will look at the different forms of pastoral and spiritual care provided by professionals, note the distinguishing characteristics, and explore some ethical issues pursuant to spiritual direction in particular.

Pastoral Care

"Pastoral care" is the broad term used by mainline Protestants to encompass any caring action performed by pastors and other recognized religious leaders who minister by virtue of their ordination or office on behalf of a community of faith. This is the basic ministry of care and support extended to all members of a congregation. Long before Alice or John sought a private appointment, Sarah had been providing pastoral care to each of them. In carrying out her general ministerial functions in the church—preaching, worship, committees, church gatherings—she has provided space for each of them to experience God in their lives. Further, she has communicated to them that she is a caring and trustworthy pastor with whom they can share their personal concerns. Both Alice and John find her approachable.

When they seek a one-on-one conversation, however, they

61

enter another level of pastoral care. The traditional Latin term for pastoral care—*cura animarum*—means "care of souls."[1] It distinguishes pastoral care from the interventions offered by the secular helping professions, for example, social workers, psychologists, or psychiatrists. Pastoral care acknowledges the religious nature of life's value and significance by placing its form of care in the context of ultimate meaning. Acts of pastoral care are performed within the horizon of God's caring love, usually in the name of or on behalf of a community of faith.

Since the Latin *cura* includes not only the notion of "caring" but also the notion of "healing," the phrase "cure of souls" is often used interchangeably with "care of souls." Pastoral care typically includes one or both of two essential elements: it can be oriented toward cure (healing) or toward growth. Pastoral counseling and spiritual direction are specialized ministries encompassed by the broad term "pastoral care." Pastoral counseling is primarily directed toward healing, and spiritual direction toward growth. Yet each practice may involve elements of the other. Healing usually involves some form of spiritual or psychological growth needed to overcome a crisis or painful circumstance. Spiritual growth may result from the resolution of emotional or spiritual pain, but often the desire for spiritual growth can be a response to a longing for life's deeper meaning.

When Sarah is approached by Alice and John, then, her first task is to discern what form of pastoral care is needed for each. Sarah is especially capable of making these recommendations because of her own interest and training in both spiritual direction and pastoral counseling. In John's case the desire for spiritual growth seems to be motivated by his past experience of a meaningful prayer life and his desire to touch those depths once again. Alice, on the other hand, is experiencing pain in the form of anxiety—dis-ease—and may benefit from a form of pastoral care focused more on healing. Sarah thus decides that spiritual direction is most appropriate for John, and that pastoral counseling is most appropriate for Alice.

Pastoral Counseling

Pastoral counseling developed as a specific type of pastoral conversation used for the care of souls. This ministry has been understood in much of this century as care of people who are troubled. It focuses on the healing aspect of pastoral care. John Patton defines pastoral counseling as "a specialized type of pastoral care offered in response to individuals, couples, or families who are experiencing and able to articulate the pain in their lives and willing to seek pastoral help in order to deal with it."[2]

The traditional biblical image invoked to describe this type of pastoral conversation is that of the shepherd seeking the lost sheep. This image reflects the Protestant approach emergent in the 1920s in the United States that viewed pastoral care and counseling as ministering to the ill or wounded. The lost sheep image also unfortunately conveys an inherent paternalism, as one envisions a benevolent shepherd reaching down to meet the needs of the lost soul. Moreover, it can be used to support approaches to pastoral counseling that focus on the individual in isolation from family systems and the wider social context.

In today's world new metaphors are needed to convey the nature of the ministry of pastoral counseling. Archie Smith, Jr., uses the metaphor of the deep river to explore how the "deepening of spiritual resources in both church and family can... play a crucial role in therapy with African Americans."[3] This image of the deep river—with its enigmatic meaning expressed so powerfully in the African American spiritual "Deep River"—points to the journey that lies ahead for those who choose to navigate the depths of their lives. The metaphor suggests that to investigate and contemplate the river one must see it in its context, understand the many elements that contribute to it, and explore the unfathomable depths to which it reaches. At a minimum this means seeing the individual within the family and organizational systems that give shape to life.

Today it is usually assumed that pastoral counseling occurs in the office of a religious counselor with an individual, couple, partnership, or family. However, pastors may also lead counseling groups—for example, grief recovery, marriage preparation, survivors of incest. Whether it is done with individuals or groups, it is crucial that pastoral counseling attend to family systems and the wider social context. Crises, pain, and conflict are not simply the results of individuals making poor choices in their lives. Pain is perpetuated when injustices are explicitly or implicitly supported by surrounding cultural systems and allowed to continue unchecked. As we struggle in a pluralistic world to learn to live together with some level of social justice and social harmony, issues surrounding race, class, gender, sexual orientation, and nationalism must be addressed. As issues are explored within the framework of family systems and the wider social context, the artificial distinctions that divide pastoral concerns from social justice issues are dissolved.

This is a demanding task. Joretta L. Marshall speaks of the challenges facing pastoral counselors:

> If pastoral representatives are to face the complexities of a postmodern world, they need a rich and multiperspectival theological vantage point. Caregivers must be as versed in the literature of traditional and today's theology as they are in psychodynamic theory. A shift in emphasis from the one-on-one counseling modality to a genuine pastoral theological concern is imperative for congregations.[4]

The shift in focus from primarily psychological dynamics to theological concerns that address the social and cultural context of pastoral counseling broadens our understanding of the shoals hidden beneath the deep river.[5] The context in which Sarah exercises pastoral care thus includes growing awareness of the importance of social location and context for understanding parishioners' needs as well as the role of the various family and social systems that shape life in her community.

Spiritual Direction

Pastoral care can not only address the needs of those who are hurting, but can also support those seeking spiritual growth. This move to broaden the Protestant approach to pastoral care is reflected in the changed subtitle of a book still used in many introductory pastoral care courses, Howard Clinebell's *Basic Types of Pastoral Care and Counseling.*[6] The original 1966 subtitle was *New Resources for Ministering to the Troubled.* When this book was revised and republished in 1984, the subtitle was changed to *Resources for the Ministry of Healing and Growth.* The book reflects the growing interest in forms of care that serve those who seek to deepen their spiritual lives.

A commitment to the ministry of spiritual direction is occurring in mainline Protestant churches in response to the widespread desire for spiritual growth. The precise form this will take is in flux, but a number of types and modes of spiritual direction are emerging. Educational opportunities for formal training are expanding. We will look at the nature of this ministry and turn to the case of John to explicate some of the contrasts between pastoral counseling and spiritual direction.

Spiritual direction is not a new term in the Roman Catholic tradition. In its pre–Vatican II manifestation, spiritual direction emphasized the importance of confession, penance, and obedience. Priests or leaders in religious orders generally provided the spiritual guidance for those who were in some sense under their authority. The relationship was often seen as father-child, superior-subject, or director-confessor.[7] The terms "spiritual director" and "directee" owe their origin to this time when the authority of the director was thought to require obedience from the directee.

Since Vatican II, spiritual direction has undergone a number of significant transformations in the Roman Catholic Church. These transformations are further intensified as mainline Protestants become increasingly involved in the ministry of spiritual direction. Today there is considerable freedom in the selection of directors for both Protestants and Catholics. In most instances the traditional distinctions of lay, ordained, religious, married, single, male, or female no longer prescribe the perimeters of those selecting a director.[8] Given the move away from authority-based approaches to spiritual direction, the term "spiritual guidance" is a more adequate description of the actual ministry. However, in this book we will follow the established custom of using the terms "director" and "directee" in the awareness that they denote a relationship defined not by clerical authority but by the gifts and graces of spiritual guidance.

Today many names are used for those who provide spiritual guidance, including but not limited to "spiritual director," "spiritual guide," "spiritual friend," "soul mate," "coach," and "companion." Each of these terms suggests a sometimes subtly different context for sharing one's spiritual life. Formal spiritual direction typically involves a director who is trained or certified to work with a directee in a relationship structured around one fifty-minute session a month. The one-on-one conversation is traditional. Here the director is typically a person with some experience on the spiritual journey. Both the director and the directee affirm that the ultimate spiritual director of both their lives is God.[9] The frequency of meeting is different if the directee goes on a directed retreat. Although some Roman Catholic religious orders require their members to participate in thirty-day retreats at some point during their ministries, Protestants more commonly spend two to seven days in quiet at intervals appropriate to their needs. In these settings persons may meet with their director daily.

Because of the wide variety of models used for spiritual direction, it is not easy to provide a uniform definition that adequately encompasses them all. However, a general definition is offered by several commentators responding to the efforts of Spiritual Directors International to develop a code of ethics for spiritual direction. One suggests that spiritual direction is "companionship with another person or group through which the Holy One shines with wisdom, encouragement and discernment."[10] Another suggests that at the root of spiritual direction is "an opportunity to reflect intentionally on one's relationship with God in the presence of another who listens with compassion."[11]

Because spiritual direction works not on people's pain but on their growing edges, the power imbalance between director and directee is often less than with the counselor and counselee relationship. The primary focus of the conversation is on the directee's agenda and experience. However, power is still an issue. Indeed, one commentator notes that as directees open the stories of their lives, they become very vulnerable, so that how the director holds power is crucial.[12] The director is assumed to have knowledge of a variety of spiritual practices, including prayer techniques and traditions. As a result of this experience the director may help the directee avoid common pitfalls as well as aid in enhancing moments rich in meaning. The director helps the directee discern where God's transforming love is at work in the variety of arenas illuminated by the grid (see chapter 1). God's presence is normally acknowledged in the sessions symbolically through the use of a candle, empty chair, icon, or some other object with religious significance.

As opposed to a spiritual *director,* spiritual *friends* are usually peers who get together on a regular and established basis to discuss their spiritual lives. With these conversations each person has agenda time for the purpose of mutual support in faith and accountability to spiritual disciplines and goals. Input from trusted peers can be most helpful when discerning the movement of God's transforming love in one's life. This opportunity for sharing, for mutual support, constructive guidance, and accountability may occur between individuals or in small groups. Those who do spiritual sharing as "soul mates" often have deep, abiding relationships that last a lifetime. The sharing that occurs between persons who consider themselves soul mates often has a deeper level of intimacy than that among friends or peers.[13]

Although Protestants are not as familiar as Roman Catholics with the term "spiritual direction," providing spiritual guidance has long been a concern of Protestant churches and movements. When Protestants largely abandoned the practice of private confession to a priest, it meant that spiritual guidance was less likely to occur in an individual context. In the Protestant tradition spiritual guidance has most often occurred in small groups. Protestants were very concerned about the movement of the spirit in everyday life, but they believed this could best be discerned in small groups committed to Bible study, prayer, religious education, and public worship. For example, John Wesley's Holy Club is a marvelous case of a community committed to spiritual growth and nurture. While at Oxford University, John and his brother Charles formed this small group, which met for support, accountability, and personal sharing. They had a covenant to celebrate Communion twice weekly, pray and read the Bible daily, engage in self-examination, fast, and do works of mercy among the poor. Thus spiritual guidance was provided in the context of the small group, fitting the model of spiritual friends.

We believe that as the interest in spiritual direction continues to grow, mainline Protestant pastors will reflect more systematically on their role as spiritual directors of their congregations and of small groups within their congregations. Spiritual direction training programs are increasingly helping clergy understand their role in helping a congregation discern how God's transforming love is at work in their church as an institution (including small groups and meetings of church committees) and in the wider society.

Pastoral Counseling Versus Spiritual Direction

Some important differences between the two modes of pastoral care are immediately apparent: pastoral counseling tends to focus on healing wounds, whereas spiritual direction focuses on growth; pastoral counseling typically involves weekly sessions, whereas spiritual direction generally involves monthly sessions; pastoral counseling continues until the issues of concern reach some state of resolution (this may require few or many sessions), whereas spiritual direction is generally an ongoing relationship focused on personal growth. We can strengthen the contrast by illustrating why Sarah decided that pastoral counseling was appropriate for Alice, while spiritual direction was appropriate for John.

Let us begin with Alice. First, Alice came with a concern focused in a specific problem: her daughter's behavior and its implications for Alice's understanding of God. Alice was troubled, hurting, and in need of healing. Second, pastoral counseling, conducted in weekly sessions of fifty minutes, would provide Alice the necessary support to work on the family issues related to her daughter's behavior and on the faith issues that emerged from this family crisis. Where there is such a degree of crisis and pain the security that weekly sessions provide is an important aspect of the healing process. Third, Sarah knew that a pastoral counselor with training in marriage and family matters would likely suggest meeting together with all the members of Alice's family. Using a family therapy mode rather than an individual counseling mode would help the entire family address the situation. Fourth, Sarah knew that most pastoral counselors would also feel comfortable talking with Alice about the impact of the family situation on her understanding and experience of God. Although Alice's family problems were her presenting concern, Sarah anticipated that being able to deal with spiritual concerns in the context of the pastoral counseling would be helpful to Alice.

A fifth factor, the use of transference by the pastoral counselor to facilitate healing, would be enhanced by the bond that can be established through weekly sessions. Transference occurs when the person seeking counseling transfers well-established but often unrecognized feelings toward other authority figures (often parents) to the pastoral counselor.

When an increasingly deep bond of trust develops over time (normally requiring more than three or four counseling sessions) between the pastoral counselor and the counselee, these feelings emerge spontaneously. Healing occurs as the pastoral counselor accepts and deals constructively—explicitly or implicitly—with these dynamics. The feelings transferred are often varied and complex, usually ones that have not been accepted by parents or early authority figures. They often include anger, hopelessness, guilt, sexual attraction, resentment. When confined to a context where they can be appropriately expressed in the presence of a skilled counselor, the resolution of these dynamics makes a strong contribution to health and wholeness.

When John approached Sarah requesting a personal conversation, she agreed to meet with him two or three times to help him determine what course of action would be most helpful. On the basis of the following observations she decided to recommend that he enter a spiritual direction group that was active in the congregation. First, John approached her not in pain or turmoil, but with a desire to develop his spiritual life more fully. Sarah's personal experience and professional training in a spiritual direction program made her aware of the role spiritual direction can exercise in the lives of those who wish to draw specifically upon their spiritual longings and practices for growth.

Second, John wanted to work explicitly with the religious dimension of his life. In contrast to pastoral counseling where religious concerns may remain largely implicit depending on the nature of the issue, in spiritual direction the religious life of the directee is an explicit concern. For those like John who have an active prayer life, the contexts and experiences of prayer may be the basis for much of the encounter. For those without an active prayer life who do not engage in any spiritual disciplines, the conversation would likely focus on their hopes and desires as well as on things done occasionally or sporadically to nurture their spirits. It is important to remember that most people do things to nurture their spirits even if they have not conceptualized what they do as a religious activity. For example, walks in nature, time alone on the beach, and thinking about those one loves while doing dishes can be deeply spiritual activities. In spiritual direction people are encouraged to deepen their understanding of God's presence in their daily activities and in the wider world.

Third, John was prepared to accept responsibility for his own growth. Since spiritual direction is frequently conducted at monthly intervals, a considerable amount of spiritual and emotional material is processed and integrated without the input from a spiritual director. Sarah recognized from her meetings with John that the dynamics of transference toward a pastoral counselor would not be a primary source of growth for John. In spiritual direction both the director and the directee keep the focus of the growth anchored in the directee's experiential relationship with the divine. As the directee moves to the depths of the holy within, the director will help the directee attend to those depths, but the transference will be focused on the relationship with God.

Having determined that John was an appropriate candidate for spiritual direction, Sarah offered him a few options for exploring his spiritual growth, including a small group in the congregation committed to spiritual nurture. This was a group of six people who met monthly to check in with one another and nurture their spiritual lives. This group was usually open to new members if they perceived that the person was serious about the task and willing to commit to the group meetings. Sarah also knew personally a Roman Catholic sister who would be willing to work one-on-one with John if he preferred that format.

In short, both pastoral counseling and spiritual direction are forms of pastoral caregiving, but these forms have important structural differences: one focuses on healing, the other on growing; one meets more frequently, the other less; and in each process the dynamics of transference are focused differently.

Having noted some differences that tend to distinguish pastoral counseling from spiritual direction, it is also necessary to point out that a considerable degree of flexibility exists in structuring any specific situation. For example, spiritual directors may meet weekly with directees if spiritually or emotionally challenging material is emerging in process. During guided retreats—normally held in retreat settings—directors may meet daily with directees for the duration of the retreat (for example, a weekend, one week, two weeks, or thirty days). Pastoral counselors and pastors providing short-term care may also see people two or three or more times a week. For example, in cases where there has been trauma caused by a sudden death, injury, accident, loss, or problematic medical diagnosis, people may need more frequent pastoral care during the acute stage of the crisis. On the other hand, pastoral counselors frequently extend the interval between sessions as a client nears the end of the pastoral counseling process. They may meet every two weeks for a month or two and then monthly for a session or two depending on the needs of the client and the counseling style of the counselor. It is also necessary to acknowledge that the focus on healing in the pastoral counseling process and on growth during spiritual direction does not mean that healing and growth are mutually exclusive categories. Healing normally involves growth, and growth often brings about some degree of healing. The point is that it is the *primary* focus on healing or on growth that distinguishes the two modalities of pastoral care. These structural differences with their flexible boundaries mean that the ethical issues raised by spiritual direction will not adequately be addressed by simply applying models derived from pastoral counseling modalities. It is to these ethical issues that we now turn.

Ethical Reflections

A number of ethical issues emerge when pastors provide spiritual guidance. We deal here with only a sample. They are ethical issues raised by pastors doing spiritual direction, and ones that emerge from the struggles of groups such as Spiritual Directors International to develop guidelines for practice.

Boundaries and Dual Relationships

As noted in chapter 2, the question of boundaries and dual relationships has been a contested one in clergy ethics. This issue emerges again when we look at spiritual care direction. Recall, for example, that having chosen pastoral counseling for Alice, Sarah decided to refer Alice to someone else and not to offer extended pastoral counseling, even though she has a pastoral counseling practice. Many people think that long-term, more sustained forms of care and counseling should not be offered to members of one's own congregation, for a variety of reasons.

First, in a longer-term pastoral counseling relationship the interpersonal transference dynamics between the pastoral counselor and the counselee are often an important source of healing. These dynamics are most appropriately dealt with in the structured context of the counseling session. If the pastor and parishioners have a number of opportunities for interaction in other settings (for example, church business meetings or social functions), transference dynamics derived from the counseling relationship can arise in these other settings. If this occurs, there is potential for harm for the counselee, for the pastor, and for other members of the church.

Second, Sarah's decision reflects the predominant view today that pastors should avoid dual relationships with parishioners. Within the context of the church community her opportunities for ministry may be diminished if she is seen to have "favorites" or "special friends" within the congregation. Congregants need to believe they have the potential to be on equal footing with other church members. Pastors who form special attachments to specific people within a congregation often jeopardize their ability to minister to the needs of the wider church community. Such attachments may make other members reluctant to share confidences with a pastor they fear may inadvertently share personal information with special friends. Parishioners who feel insecure or perceive others as having the pastor's ear may act out in decision processes within committee structures of the church.[14] For example, a parishioner who feels insecure or neglected and who believes a particular church committee chairperson is a personal friend of the pastor may feel resentful, wanting equal time from the pastor. This resentment may be expressed not directly toward the pastor or the chairperson, but by opposition to the guidance they provide or decisions they make. Here we see that opposition may arise not because the insecure parishioner truly objects to the guidance or decisions provided, but because he or she resents the friendship between the pastor and the committee chairperson.

Third, in relationships of unequal power—where one party is responsible for assisting another—there is evidence that not maintaining proper boundaries has all too often resulted in sexual harassment or abuse of the less powerful person. Literature in the area of sexual abuse and exploitation confirms that establishing clear boundaries for professional practice is one avenue for preventing such violations. Maintaining clear boundaries not only keeps the caregiver aware of ethical guidelines, it also helps prevent the possibility that actions of either the pastor or the counselee could be misinterpreted. The therapeutic bond that develops between those working together with long-term counseling agendas fosters levels of intimacy that can more easily be subject to misinterpretation if the pastoral counselor and the client have associations in contexts where other power relations apply. In the current context where sexual abuse remains an important concern, for moral as well as legal reasons it is often better to err on the side of restraint by maintaining clear boundaries, than to chance blurring them out of a misguided or ill-conceived desire to be helpful.

The Code of Ethics of the American Association of Pastoral

Counselors and the Spiritual Directors International Guidelines for Ethical Conduct both argue for avoiding dual relationships, maintaining appropriate boundaries, and averting unethical sexual behavior.

> We recognize the trust placed in and unique power of the therapeutic relationship. While acknowledging the complexity of some pastoral relationships, we avoid exploiting the trust and dependency of clients. We avoid those dual relationships with clients (e.g., business or close personal relationships) which could impair our professional judgement, compromise the integrity of the treatment, and/or use the relationship for our own gain.[15]

> All forms of sexual behavior or harassment with clients are unethical, even when a client invites or consents to such behavior or involvement. Sexual behavior is defined as, but not limited to, all forms of overt and covert seductive speech, gestures, and behavior as well as physical contact of a sexual nature; harassment is defined as but not limited to, repeated comments, gestures or physical contacts of a sexual nature.[16]

> Spiritual Directors honor the dignity of the directee by: . . . c) recognizing the imbalance of power in the spiritual direction relationship and taking care not to exploit it, d) establishing and maintaining appropriate physical and psychological boundaries with the directee, e) refraining from sexualized behavior, including, but not limited to manipulative, abusive or coercive words or actions toward a directee.[17]

In short, in recent years a wide societal consensus has emerged that maintaining clear boundaries is useful in professional relationships to protect both the person seeking assistance and the professional providing it. If a pastor sees members of the congregation for long-term pastoral counseling or spiritual direction, the risk increases that these boundaries may become blurred.

However, not everyone agrees that it is possible or necessary to avoid dual relationships in pastoral care, especially in spiritual direction. As we saw in chapter 2, different models of ministry can lead to different interpretations of appropriate boundaries or limits on relationships between pastor and parishioner. The *Code of Ethics for Spiritual Directors* promulgated by the Center for Sacred Psychology, for example, suggests that dual relationships should not be automatically prohibited in spiritual direction, for two reasons. First, the chronicles of spiritual direction are "noteworthy" for the number of hats that people have worn. Second, the presence of God as a "third person" in the relationship means that rules will often be broken, as this is what God does![18]

In short, boundaries may not need to be as "tight" around spiritual direction as around pastoral counseling. Spiritual direction sessions are not to the same degree a ministry to the hurting or vulnerable (although people in direction can be dealing with hurts and be vulnerable). And since the directee accepts more responsibility for growth and meets only monthly with the director, transference functions in a different way. Whereas in pastoral counseling the transference onto the counselor is an important source of healing, in spiritual direction transference occurs in the relationship of the directee with the divine rather than with the human director. Less frequent sessions also minimize transference between the directee and director (although certainly there is some transference occurring when people of unequal power work together). Where transference is likely to be minimal, it may not be unethical for pastors to hold dual relationships with parishioners.

As a result, some directors work with people with whom they have relationships in other contexts. Depending on the nature of the relationship between two people, they may openly discuss and acknowledge that they have a dual relationship and decide to proceed with spiritual direction. Spiritual Directors International was careful to note that its code of ethics provides *guidelines*. This was to reflect the varied ways in which direction occurs and the necessity to recognize that the ethical issues are often specific to the given context. In general, where spiritual direction is given once a month or less and where there is no evidence of mental illness or personality structures that would make transference a problem, a pastor may ethically provide long-term spiritual direction to parishioners, so long as she or he is also attentive to any possibility of jealousy or changed dynamics in the congregation as a whole.

Competence and Context

Nonetheless, we also recognize that context matters. In the cases of Sarah, Alice, and John we had an ideal situation—a pastor who understood the nature and value of pastoral counseling and spiritual direction as well as pastoral care. Frequently, however, clergy do not work in settings where they have colleagues with specialized training in pastoral counseling and spiritual direction. The majority of clergy work in small communities or rural settings where they may have few colleagues to whom they can make referrals. What is a pastor to do as the "only game in town" when *not* specially trained in spiritual direction?

Ethical guidelines for professionals always require that professionals recognize their limitations. By extension, clergy are responsible for practicing within their range of competence. We experience something of a dilemma here. On the one hand, we believe that caring and sensitive religious professionals who have little formal training may nonetheless be excellent spiritual guides. On the other hand, we are mindful of what the Spiritual Directors International Ethics Task Force called "spiritual pride"—the tendency to believe that because one is called, one automatically possesses special gifts and spiritual uprightness.[19] Both authors of this volume teach in fields (ethics and spirituality) that are prone to having untrained people claim expertise. This probably makes us a bit unduly leery of people without expert training.

Consequently, we generally think that clergy should be careful about claiming expertise in spiritual direction unless they have had the opportunity for specialized training and work. For example, directees on the spiritual journey may experience what spiritual directors know as "the dark night of the soul" when the spiritual life seems especially arid and God seems to be absent. Depending on the intensity of this state it may be confused with clinical depression. Trained pastoral counselors and spiritual directors need to know the signs and characteristics that differentiate the darkness of depression from the dark night of the soul. Directees or clients who need psychiatric or medical treatment to prevent further depression or suicide are ill-served if their professional caregivers do not attend to the signs and symptoms of clinical depression.[20]

Clergy need to know how to make appropriate referrals when serving those who need assistance beyond their capabilities.[21] Knowing other professionals who are sensitive to religious concerns and who can offer medical, legal, psychiatric, psychological, social, nutritional, and other services is useful. Since religious leaders remain the front line of assistance for great numbers of people in our society, most clergy take seriously their ministry of referral.

Nonetheless, there are circumstances in which clergy do not have opportunities for specialized training and cannot easily refer people to others who have been specially trained. Many smaller or more geographically remote communities do not have access to such resources. Sometimes a few meetings with a parishioner may address the concerns raised. Sometimes a parishioner can be referred to a small group of fellow seekers and spiritual friends. But sometimes, there is no one else available. Having an abiding concern for people and an ability to be an attentive, active listener are required. Specialized training in spiritual direction is not necessarily required. In these instances, we believe this is a judgment call based on a number of factors that have to be weighed in each situation. Does the pastor maintain an active prayer life? Does she have peers in ministry who can help supervise the spiritual direction she provides to others? Spiritual directors who do not attend to their own spiritual development eventually lose the relationship with the divine that is crucial to the spiritual direction process. Directees are seldom helped by directors who are careless with their own spiritual issues or who do not submit their own work as a director to the guidance and accountability of peers. Every professional code of ethics requires not only that professionals recognize their limits, but also that they work to maintain and increase their skills. This applies in ministry as elsewhere.

The Grid

The grid provides a systematic means for exploring the various venues where God's transforming love is at work in daily life. We have talked about this from the perspective of seeing the multifaceted way in which God seeks to transform the world. The grid, by providing a lens for exploring God's activity, also raises significant ethical issues.

If a directee focuses on the intrapersonal aspects of divine activity in daily life she may well be growing personally. Such personal growth is crucial for nurturing an experiential relationship with the holy. We believe, however, that directors do have a responsibility to notice if a person keeps his or her relationship with God focused in only one or two aspects of the grid. Doing so raises some crucial issues about one's willingness to see God's wider activity. Failure to see can have important ethical implications for personal relationships, structural aspects of life, and the environment.

For someone who has never considered the wider arenas of God's activity, the links between personal devotion and social justice may not be seen unless they are lifted up by a director. In the same fashion a person who has been highly involved in social justice projects with little time for personal reflection may not realize that personal transformations when noticed can have a profound impact on the way in which the person understands not only justice issues but also

79

the appropriate means to address them. Many of our great social reformers have had well-established devotional practices that have kept them open to fresh energy and new insights for their tasks.

Dealing with Differences

Spiritual directors normally spend at least one session with potential directees to discern if the two persons are being led to work together. Typically the two persons will meet, get a sense of the feel of the relationship, and agree to pray about it during the interval before they are to meet again. This provides an opportunity not only to see if they believe they can work together, but also to gain a sense of God's leading in the process. Directors and directees have issues that emerge from their own psychological and spiritual histories. Sometimes such issues lead each party to ongoing growth while at other times these issues may prevent the creation of a context where each person is free to listen to God's spirit. Two respondents in our survey raised a question about working with people with whom they are uncomfortable for some reason.

In one case, a lesbian woman sought help from a heterosexual director, whose tradition and training had left her still somewhat uncomfortable dealing with homosexuality. The Code of Ethics for Spiritual Directors developed by the Center for Sacred Psychology suggests that directors may screen prospective directees.[22] For instance, directors may choose not to take on a directee if both of them have a similar unresolved personal issue. Thus, it would be acceptable for the director to refuse to take on someone if the director thinks that her unresolved issues will make it difficult for her to be a good director. However, the guidelines of Spiritual Directors International also require that directors show respect for all persons and not discriminate. Thus, a director needs to be clear that she is avoiding a prospective client not because of prejudice, but out of a genuine concern that she might not be helpful to the directee. In light of the fact that homophobia raises serious justice issues, she also needs to continue her own professional development to eradicate homophobia.

Moreover, once someone has been taken under direction, that person must not be abandoned. Hence, if the director does not learn that the directee is lesbian until after a relationship has been established, she may not simply terminate the relationship. In this case, it becomes incumbent upon her to deal with any lingering prejudices that may make it difficult for her to do good work with the directee.

In the second case, the tables were turned: a straight woman sought help from a lesbian director, not knowing that the director was lesbian. The director then had to decide whether to divulge her sexual orientation. The ethical dilemma arises because she is bound both by duties of helping the directee and by duties of truth-telling. Truth-telling would require that she tell the directee, but doing so may not be helpful to her client. We would argue for the priority of truth-telling in this instance. Not only does it generally take precedence over doing good (indeed, for Kant truth-telling was a duty of "perfect" obligation that could never be broken), but there are justice issues that support truth-telling as well: homophobia contributes to injustice in the world. Sadly, however, we have to report that when the director divulged her sexual orientation, hoping that the relationship was strong enough to bear the news, the directee disappeared. Since spiritual direction focuses on growth rather than on healing, we can only hope that the directee was not harmed by the information and has subsequently found someone else who will enable her growth—including using the grid to require that she look at homophobia and its effects on her relationship with God.

Fees

Many directors have struggled over the question of compensation for their work. The role of fees and their relationship to professional training and the context of the ministry is a vexing one. Counseling centers that provide spiritual direction usually require fees to support the center. Those in ministries where revenue comes through contributions to a wider ministry often do not charge fees. People who are not formally trained in spiritual direction usually do not charge. Spiritual friends, soul mates, and groups usually do not have fees. However, as spiritual direction becomes more popular in Protestant circles, it is to be expected that more clergy may wish to make their living as spiritual directors and therefore will find it necessary to charge fees.

They should be forewarned that there are legal implications to accepting fees. Charging fees implies that one is providing a "professional" service and should have the requisite training, supervision, and structured practice. In this litigious society, people who are professionally trained and charge fees are subject to closer scrutiny from a legal vantage point. We raised at the outset a case study in which an insurance company was leery about providing malpractice insurance to a denomination that had not set standards for "spiritual direction" offered by its clergy. When clergy or religious leaders claim to be spiritual directors, there may be legal liabilities for them or for their denominations.

When is it appropriate to charge fees? One very wise pastor has a saying that we appreciate: "My love is free; my time isn't." Where one's time is covered by the general job description in a church, it is already paid. Where one's time is not covered by the general job description in a church, it is not already paid and should be compensated. Here, weddings might provide a model. Performing weddings is part of a pastor's ministry to a church, but we do not expect pastors to perform all weddings without compensation. Certainly, fees are charged those *outside* the membership of the church. The same might apply to spiritual direction. Thus, it would not be inappropriate for Sarah to charge a modest fee when she does spiritual direction for those who are not church members, but it would be inappropriate for her to charge a fee for leading a spiritual growth group within the church. In any event, all fees and compensation should be clearly discussed and agreed upon before a spiritual direction relationship is established.

Follow-up

Several directors struggled with the question of what to do when a directee cancels appointments. Indeed, several told stories of directees who made one appointment after another and then canceled. Should they call the directee? Should they assume that the directee was taking care of himself or herself, and that it was not a problem? Should they be assertive or persistent in trying to get the directee to come in for a session? Should they charge a fee for their time, if the directee did not cancel early enough for them to fill the slot?

This is one place where structural differences between counseling and spiritual direction become important. Since counseling focuses on healing wounds, a missed session is typically indicative that the person is beginning to confront hurting places. For additional healing to take place, it is important that the counseling not be interrupted. However, since spiritual direction focuses on growing edges, a missed session does not hold the same import. It is possible, of course, that growth is beginning to be painful. But spiritual direction is understood to be more under the control of the directee. Therefore, if a directee wants to pause for a time, there is likely little harm done. Sessions can begin again when the directee is ready.

However, directors do have to honor and respect themselves, and are also within proper ethical conduct when they require directees to honor and respect them. If fees are normally charged for the session, and the cancellation is not due to an emergency and does not give sufficient time to fill the slot, it is not inappropriate to charge the fee. It is also not inappropriate to terminate the spiritual direction relationship when one party has been consistently disrespectful of the other's time and efforts. In this case, we might say that the directee has abandoned the director, rather than the reverse.

CHAPTER 4

Spiritual Care
in Congregations

Mark Palmer has been the pastor of Third Avenue
United Church of Christ for several months. He was
excited when he made the move to Third Avenue
because of the racial and cultural diversity among its members. A highly educated core of leaders associated with a near-
by church-related college have worked hard to make this a
welcoming community. This church is well positioned to
extend its community outreach.

Two weeks ago Mark preached a sermon titled "Spirituality
and Social Justice: The Tie That Binds." In it, he spoke about
the way people "miss the mark" when they fail to see the
connections between their spiritual lives and their social
actions. At one point he spoke of the failure to listen carefully
for God's action in everyday life. He said, "We know that evil
exists in our world, when injustice, hatred and prejudice go
unchallenged. Our sin is not listening for God's claim on our
lives. Our sin is forgetting that God cares deeply about our
daily activities."

Later that week at a meeting of the Pastor Parish Relations Committee, Mark was asked not to preach about "sin." It was explained to him that talk of sin was outdated. Such preaching would make people feel guilty and, as one member said, "Guilt doesn't do anyone any good." Mark explained that he believed sin was an important theological concept and argued that Christians need to understand the presence of evil in our lives and in the world. He said he does not attempt to "instill guilt in people" and certainly in pastoral counseling does not try to make people "feel guilty," but he thinks the pastor should be allowed to speak about sin from the pulpit. The council said they understood his position, but hoped he would heed their advice. They feared their community would lose its welcoming reputation if sin became a significant agenda item of sermons.

This case raises a number of ethical issues. If Mark speaks of sin in a congregation that does not want him to discuss it, is he so out of step with his denomination or congregation that this is not the right church for him? Is he being spiritually abusive to speak of sin in his sermons? Is it wrong for a pastor to exercise this kind of leadership? Is he guilty of spiritual neglect if he heeds the advice of the Pastor Parish Relations Committee and does *not* speak of sin? How can we develop an ethical framework for the myriad ways in which parish clergy provide spiritual care?

The task is complicated by the fact that the role of parish clergy is notoriously ill-defined and open-ended. This makes ethical analysis problematic, as we saw in chapter 2. In parish ministry, few clergy consider themselves as providing explicit spiritual direction. Rather, clergy see themselves as providing "spiritual care" in a rather wide range of settings:

- Worship, especially preaching;
- Education classes for children, youth, and adults;
- Counseling and pastoral care situations;
- Special occasions such as weddings, memorial services, and baptisms;
- Church board meetings and committees;

- Informal settings such as passing in the hallway.

Indeed, as one pastor said when we asked her where she provides spiritual care, "I try to sneak it in everywhere!"[1] Each setting may generate Its own ethical dilemmas. Preaching may generate concerns about what is appropriate proclamation of the Word: Is it acceptable to preach "hell, fire, and brimstone," or should the message be exclusively one of love, forgiveness, and acceptance? Both content and delivery style may raise issues regarding appropriate "fit" with the setting, congregation, and basic message of the faith, as seems to have happened in Mark's case.

Other settings create their own dilemmas. Education classes provide unique opportunities for mutual challenge of perspectives and presuppositions. Are there limits to the kinds or amount of challenge that clergy should use toward parishioners? How does one juggle the needs of those with varying degrees of education and sophistication in order to provide appropriate spiritual care to each? Special occasions such as weddings and baptisms are often fraught with extra emotional meaning for people, and good spiritual care may require deft handling of that meaning.

We cannot provide a complete overview here of all the arenas and types of dilemmas encountered. Instead, we will focus on some that clergy raised with us and some that the literature suggests may be significant.

Ethical Quandaries of Clergy

Clergy identify a number of issues that present ethical dilemmas in the provision of spiritual care in the church. From these, we have chosen the following for elaboration.[2]

When to Tell People "This Is Not the Right Church for You"

Almost all clergy at some time confront the problem of a misfit between a parishioner and the church body as a whole.

Sometimes this is because a parishioner's stance on an ethical issue (for example, acceptance or rejection of gay and lesbian church members) does not fit the stance of the congregation as a whole. Sometimes it is a theological issue, in which a parishioner's understanding of God is considerably different from the understanding preached and accepted by the church body. Sometimes it is a personality problem, such as a negative person whose energy is spent draining the church and its members and blocking programs and progress.

Whatever the reason for the misfit, most clergy find it hard to ask someone to *leave* the church. Asking someone to leave the church feels wrong to clergy, who are largely geared toward wanting to bring people *into* the church. It feels to clergy as if saying "This is not the right church for you" is like saying "Go away." It feels like pushing people away from God's love. They find it incompatible with providing spiritual care. Should people ever be asked to leave the church, and, if so, when and how? Does asking someone to leave violate a fundamental duty to care for people's spirits?

Most clergy agree that there are sometimes sufficient reasons to ask a member to leave, but they do not agree as to *when* to make this move. Some see it as an issue of how to balance the needs of one individual against the needs of the larger body: Should the church be "used" as a forum to encourage spiritual growth in one whose views are different, or should the larger body be protected and sheltered from such a role? Obviously, the answer to this question will depend in part on one's ecclesiology: What is the role of the church, and what kinds of burdens should congregations be asked to carry? A guideline that many clergy seem to enact is this: if the person is not *damaging* the church, but simply *differs* from others, they will try to keep that person as part of the congregation, but if the person's disagreement takes the form of *damaging* the church body, then it is time to ask the person to leave.[3] Implicitly, clergy appear to be acting here on their mandate to protect from harm those in their charge.

Some clergy, however, experience a particular bind stemming from denominational policies. Where denominations reward—explicitly or implicitly—clergy who have large numbers of members "on the books," not only may a pastor be reluctant to move someone off the books, but the denomination may not *permit* pastors to ask members to leave. Indeed, some clergy report strong pressure to keep people on the books even when they have not been seen in many years, so that numbers appear strong for denominational purposes. We would argue that such practices violate both principles of truth-telling (or honesty in reporting) and principles of good professional conduct. There are times when someone should be asked to leave the church and their departure noted officially.

How to ask someone to leave bothered clergy less than when to ask. Clergy all agree that a request that someone leave the church needs to be handled with love—admittedly, sometimes with "tough love." The person must not be made to feel cut off from God's redemptive love, but only as one who doesn't fit well the practices and presuppositions of this particular congregation. Here, the mandate to provide spiritual care can be honored by helping the person find a more compatible church family, if possible. Where this is not possible, excommunication—pushing someone outside the communion of faith—takes on very serious dimensions.[4] Putting someone outside the purview of the church, and by implication potentially outside the purview of God's love, raises questions of spiritual abuse. We will return to these questions in chapter 6.

Where most clergy think "tough love" is adequate, Rediger offers a different perspective for dealing with members who are truly destructive. If there is genuine spiritual conflict and evil is operating, whether by design or not, Rediger suggests that only an "exorcism" will do. By exorcism he means "the casting out of evil in a specific person or persons."[5] The exorcism formula, drawn from Jesus' own ministry, is: name the demon, cast out the demon, replace the demon.[6] Although cutting off the person from the congregation altogether is the "worst possible scenario" here, Rediger argues strongly that the congregation "should not be sacrificed to an evil agenda."[7] He recommends that a team of people be assembled to confront the person using a model of intervention.[8] Mainline Protestants in general, however, are reluctant to speak of evil or of exorcism. This may be a part of our forgotten tradition that is worth some serious review.[9]

Dealing with Noncongregants Who Come for Assistance

Many clergy—perhaps especially clergywomen—have had the experience of being sought out for assistance by someone from another church or even denomination. Parishioners from more conservative churches may seek out a "liberal" pastor for advice about divorce, remarriage, or their relationship to God. For example, Joe Driskill once had the experience of serving the only relatively "liberal" parish in a geographic region. He noticed that people from other churches experiencing marital problems (including those going through a divorce) would visit his congregation while they were in turmoil. Eventually *with* the support of those in his congregation these people would move back to their own church. Similarly, parishioners from more liberal churches may seek out a conservative pastor whose theology appears more compatible with the parishioners' convictions. In either case, the pastor has a dilemma: Should I give spiritual advice to this person at all, and, if so, should I try to tailor my advice to the person's own convictions, or speak out of my own convictions?

Most clergy feel constrained to have an "open-door" policy of welcoming those who come for advice, whether or not they are church members. Indeed, many welcome the opportunity to witness to God's love as a possible mechanism for healing, mission work, or evangelism. Most feel that they should speak out of their own convictions, while being respectful of differences between their views and those of the person seeking help. "Why would they come to *me* if they didn't want to know where I stand?" queried one.

Nonetheless, some were aware that they might make it more difficult for the person to return to their own congregation, and this was troubling to clergy who value community and believe that good spiritual care takes place within a community, not just in one-to-one encounter.

Here is a place where the model of spirituality and of professional ethics may make a big difference. Under a model of "emancipatory transformation," for example, it might be right to try to move people away from their own limited experience and convictions and toward a more liberated perspective. Active intervention that urges new understandings would be not only permissible, but possibly even required. We join feminists and others who struggle for the liberation of oppressed people in seeing the importance of "conscienticization" or consciousness-raising. However, we also offer a caution: few of us can resist the idea that *our* interpretation of the gospel is "liberating." To the extent that mutuality and mutual regard should also undergird spiritual care, it will be important for clergy to try genuinely to hear and understand the stance of those who come from different backgrounds. As Driskill's experience suggests, people can be encouraged to return to their own churches or traditions, fortified by contact with something a bit different.

Dealing with Spiritual Practices (for Example, Yoga, Tai Chi) from Other Religions and Traditions

Wendy Gallagher's *Working on God* makes clear that it is not unusual today for parishioners to be experimenting with several sources of spiritual practice. Gallagher herself studied Zen Buddhism intensively, attended numerous orthodox Jewish celebrations, and considers her "dabbling" in these alternative forms of spirituality to be rather typical of the "neo-agnostic" generation. But clergy confronted by parishioners with requests to allow or even foster such eclectic spirituality may find that they have a problem: *Should* they give support to non-Christian forms of spiritual practice?

91

In *Protestant Spiritual Exercises,* Driskill offers some cautions about adopting spiritual practices as mere "techniques" for achieving a desired state of being.[10] All spiritual practices arise out of a specific context. Part of their power derives from their connection with theological roots and community history. Hence, we believe that *ethical* use of practices from other traditions must be undertaken with respect for those traditions.[11] To be respectful of a tradition is not simply to "use" it or to use part of it for our own purposes, but to honor its integrity. This means that pastors should not jump on the bandwagon of every practice that comes down the pike, but should remind parishioners of the deep meaning that they may violate by too easy an adaptation. Native American author and activist Vine Deloria once lamented the tendency of Euro-Americans to adopt a "fetish": they wear a bear symbol around their neck as though it would give them power, he railed, when in fact they have disdain for the very peoples and traditions out of which that power might arise. Similarly, an African American pastor, the Reverend Dr. J. Alfred Smith, Sr., reminds his white audiences that they may sing spirituals, but that, to him, the spirituals are not just beautiful music, but are *his story.*[12] To take a practice or tradition out of context is potentially to violate the tradition and to be disrespectful toward the people whose communities developed the tradition. This is not ethical spiritual practice.

To say this is not to say that pastors and their churches may not adopt practices that originate outside Christianity. It is to say that such practices should be adopted with care and respect and with a sense of humility: we adopt a practice precisely so that it can change *us,* not so that we can manipulate *it.* Our dialogue with other traditions is precisely in order to discover new depths in our own tradition. As Gandhi is reported to have said, if we need to leave our own religion to find the truth, we haven't discovered the truth of our own religion![13]

Dealing with the Fine Line Between Spiritual Gifts and Mental Illness

According to the California Alliance for the Mentally Ill, 40 percent of individuals experiencing emotional distress go first to their clergy rather than to physicians or psychiatrists.[14] Thus, it is to be expected that clergy would be asked to deal with people whose spiritual gifts may be accompanied by mental illness. Yet, as Rediger points out, clergy are seldom trained to deal with mental illness or aberration in long-term counseling relationships.[15]

One such case was brought to us by several clergy from a sizable congregation. A man joined their church, and it became apparent that he had considerable spiritual gifts. They invited him to lead some workshops and prayer groups. As time went on, however, it became equally apparent that his spiritual gifts were accompanied by emotional illness: he developed an obsession regarding a clergywoman, he began to act in erratic ways, he became belligerent and difficult to deal with, he accused the pastors of abuse. The pastors of this church agonized over how to deal with him. They were reluctant to shut down his spiritual growth by excluding him from prayer groups or other church events, but they also recognized that limits needed to be set in order to keep his mental and emotional aberrations from dominating church functions.

Central to their quandary was the fact that this man's spiritual gifts and his mental illness appeared to be inextricably intertwined.[16] If spirituality deals with people's basic integrity—with what makes them uniquely themselves in relation to God, self, others, and the world—then some people's spirituality may indeed be closely linked with dysfunctional psychological characteristics that are problematic if expressed in the church community. What should a pastor do when great spiritual gifts appear to be accompanied by mental illness?

Rediger notes that few churches know how to deal with people who have mental disorders. Mentally disordered people by definition do not have normal rational processes, and therefore normal rational discussion and usual church procedures may not be effective in dealing with them.[17] Rediger recommends "tough love": the application of careful policies and procedures that will allow a consensus to emerge in the church.

We stress, however, that mentally ill people are often very manipulative. In the case at hand, the man tried to convince other church members that clergy were abusing him. It may be difficult to keep the church on track and clear about what is happening. Consensus may be elusive. It may also be difficult because many people do not understand the difference between spiritual direction and psychotherapy: denominational officials in this case urged the clergyperson to undergo therapy in order to do spiritual direction. Although we applaud clergy who attend to their personal growth through ongoing therapy, we have tried to make clear in chapter 3 that there is a different base for spiritual direction than for psychotherapy or pastoral counseling. Being a good counselor may require that one remain in therapy, at least for a time. Being a good spiritual director requires attending to one's spiritual life; this may or may not involve psychotherapy or pastoral counseling.

Neglected Issues

These are issues that clergy recognize rather readily. However, the literature on clergy ethics and on contemporary church "crises" suggests that there may be other ethical issues in spiritual care that are not always recognized. Failure to recognize such issues suggests that there may in fact be a widespread problem in mainstream ministry—a problem of *spiritual neglect*.

Neglecting Family Violence

James Leehan calls family violence "a spiritual epidemic."[18] Leehan notes that family violence is the single largest cause of death among children under age five and the single largest reason women seek emergency room treatment. Most families go first to the church for help, but 85 percent of clergy in one study reported by Leehan said they questioned the reliability of the accounts they received from women and did not consider violence a sufficient cause to counsel separation or divorce. This failure to recognize the seriousness of a grave problem means that many clergy are not in fact providing good spiritual care for children, women, or men: they are neither protecting the vulnerable nor calling into account those who perpetrate violence.[19] If good spiritual care means assisting people in their spiritual growth, then both protection and safety on the one hand and confrontation and accountability on the other are an integral part of providing good spiritual care. The problem of domestic violence was flagged by Marie M. Fortune in *Sexual Violence: The Unmentionable Sin*, which remains a definitive text on this topic.[20] In recent years, churches and denominations have paid a great deal of attention to clergy sexual abuse of parishioners, but may have neglected to address the very serious issues of rampant domestic violence in our culture.

Neglecting Spiritual Growth

In *Protestant Spiritual Exercises*, Driskill noted that mainline churches have failed to nurture the spiritual lives of their members, with the result that our spiritual lives have "atrophied."[21] Driskill is not alone in making this charge. Several contemporary authors agree that mainstream churches tend to neglect spirituality altogether, to their own detriment. In *Rerouting the Protestant Mainstream*, Hadaway and Roozen argue that mainstream churches are drifting in an unreality, using outdated models of church, and failing to provide what would give people a *reason* for going to church.[22] What we need, they claim, is a "spiritually oriented mainstream church" in which the key element is worship. The church needs a clear religious identity and a coherent sense of direction. From their perspective, *"The only hope for mainstream growth is for mainstream church[es] to become more like movements and less like denominations.*"[23] Central to a revitalized mainstream church is "the reclamation of religious experience and spirituality."[24] The church, in short, must create spiritual communities that allow Christ's Spirit to live and breathe. Beliefs of church leaders are crucial at this point: Do leaders genuinely believe that God is present, and prepare for worship with this understanding?

A similar argument is made by Jeff Woods in *Congregational Megatrends*. Woods suggests that mainstream churches have talked *about* God rather than allowing parishioners to *encounter* God.[25] They need to stop being "reasonable" and allow for "mysterious" spirituality that goes beyond understanding. People both have and are hungry for direct experiences of God; it is these spiritual experiences that need to be at the core of what the church is doing. By neglecting such mystical experiences, churches are driving people away: while 73 percent of Americans say that they want a close relationship with God, only 50 percent say that being part of a church is something they greatly desire.[26]

Finally, Eugene Peterson charges that the pastor's proper task is "teaching them to pray"—that is, listening to what God is saying and forming an adequate response.[27] If clergy do not attend to this task, suggests Peterson, they do not provide proper pastoral care. Too often, he argues, clergy accept the parishioner's problem *as presented* rather than asking the parishioner to look behind the problem in order to ask what God is doing and what God wants the parishioner to do. Worship is important, because it is a time of "not-doing," when hundreds of thousands of sinners are off the streets and not getting into trouble! But worship that does not simultaneously teach us to pray—and *how* to pray—is not genuine spiritual care.

The question of how to pray may be particularly important. In *Be Careful What You Pray For . . . You Just Might Get It*, physician Larry Dossey takes up the negative side of prayer.[28] Almost all prayers, he suggests, involve a wish for the destruction of something, even if it is only cancer cells. But he notes that 5 percent of Americans admit to praying for harm to come to another; many more shout curses such as "damn you," which is implicitly a negative prayer. If we believe in the positive power of prayer, then we must also beware the negative power of prayer. (So strongly did Mary Baker Eddy believe in the power of prayer that she thought it was unethical to pray for someone without their permission.)[29] In his previous work, Dossey focused on the power of prayer to heal, but here he offers cautions based on the unpredictable nature of the outcome of prayer and its different meaning for people, and concludes with Scott Walker of the University of New Mexico School of Medicine that "people need to take responsibility for the power of their prayers."[30]

Dossey offers no advice for clergy. But we might interpret his scientific findings to offer at least the caution that clergy do need to think about the serious issues involved in teaching people to pray—how to pray, whether they should ask permission before praying for someone, and whether they should attend to the negative prayers that permeate our lives in the form of cursing and obscenities. The spirit of ill will that characterizes some people's lives may have ramifications beyond our current imaginings.

In short, these authors raise a potential challenge for mainstream clergy: Have clergy contributed to the separation between religion and spirituality by neglecting important spiritual modes and experiences and by failing to be teachers of good spiritual practices?

Neglecting Feminist Spirituality

If neglect of spiritual growth in general is an issue for ethics and spiritual care, even more pressing may be the question of feminist spirituality. In *Defecting in Place*, three noted women scholars and church leaders present the results of a national survey on how women with feminist leanings deal with their spirituality. The results of the survey are sobering at best: well over 50 percent of the respondents from *every* mainline Protestant denomination—Lutheran, Presbyterian, Methodist, Southern Baptist, American Baptist, Episcopalian, United Church of Christ, and Disciples of Christ—replied that they "often felt alienated" from their churches and denominations.[31] (Among lesbian women, the figure jumps to an alarming 86 percent.) These women feel "deprived, discounted, and stifled" in areas of significance, including spirituality.[32] Typical comments included:

> "I consider myself a very spiritual person . . . and have not found church helpful in nurturing the spiritual aspects of individuals or my journey toward wholeness."[33]

> "In my experience, the local church is largely irrelevant to spiritual growth."[34]

> "Participating in my church worship made me feel dead, sad."[35]

Some have left the church. Others have formed feminist spirituality groups, getting together for prayer, ritual, and social justice activities that become the basis for a new understanding and experience of spirituality:

> "I presently do not attend a church. My church is the women's group I attend."[36]

> "It's time for women to develop their own rituals using language and symbols that are meaningful to us, while drawing on the rich depths of our spirituality."[37]

> "How deeply I have experienced my connection with God/Universe/Goddess through the small spirituality group in which I participate."[38]

Although many women remain in the institutional church, some admit openly that it is not where they find spiritual enrichment; others "see the potential for eventually needing to reject my present church."[39]

The strength of these findings suggests that mainline churches are failing women—and men—not simply by neglecting spirituality in general, but by neglecting feminine and feminist dimensions of spirituality in particular. Winter and her colleagues consider feminist spirituality "a very serious challenge to the institutional church."[40] They argue that feminist spirituality is a new phenomenon. It includes a strong value on inclusive language for God, the use of multiple images and symbols for the godhead, a stress on women's capabilities and empowerment ("self-esteem" in Toinette Eugene's words[41]), and new forms of ritual that link women not just with traditional Christian symbols but across religious lines and with the earth itself.[42] Failure to honor these dimensions of people's spirituality will increasingly alienate women and men from the institutional church. Some women have defected and left the church; others are "defecting in place." Good spiritual care requires attention to these voices of a deep longing for better avenues to experience God.

Neglecting Stewardship

Taking a rather different tack, Robert Wuthnow suggests that churches are in financial crisis, and that this crisis is also a *spiritual* crisis occasioned at least in part by inadequate spiritual leadership by pastors. The majority of American church members are middle-class, with a median income of around $47,000.[43] They experience a lot of stress at work: 10 percent have been laid off in the last year, 8 percent have taken a pay cut, and at least 10 percent have been sexually harassed.[44] Seventy percent worry about how they are going to pay their bills. Yet only 25 percent say they pray about their finances, and only 4 percent have spoken with their pastors about financial concerns or work-related stress.[45] Indeed, more than two-thirds of the working public see money as completely separate from morals and values.[46]

In the face of this shifting social scene, church giving has declined. Nearly 50 percent of people say they would rather give to a needy family than to a church.[47] Religious giving has dropped from 3.1 percent of income in the 1960s to an average of 2.5 percent in the early 1990s.[48] As church populations age, more members are on fixed incomes. The net result is that churches are often hurting financially, and clergy are ill-prepared either to respond to the financial crisis or to understand how it relates to the spiritual well-being of their parishioners.

Studies suggest that parishioners give more, and more faithfully, when they understand giving as a form of spiritual practice and discipline, not just a response to "needs" in church or community.[49] Although clergy often feel uncomfortable talking about money, Wuthnow suggests that it is precisely the avoidance of this issue that may be failing parishioners spiritually. In other words, good spiritual care may require clergy to overcome their reluctance to deal with money as a theological issue. Wuthnow himself suggests that churches need to recapture an understanding of "stewardship" in its most basic forms. In short, Wuthnow charges that clergy are guilty of neglecting their parishioners' need to engage finances as a matter of spirituality.

Neglecting Social Justice

Wuthnow's critique implies that clergy are neglecting the larger social arena in which ministry takes place. This critique is strengthened by the analysis of another leader who raises serious questions about current "mainstream" spiritual practice in our churches. Taking a systems approach to pastoral and spiritual care in the black church in particular, Archie Smith, Jr., suggests that practices within the church must be understood as embedded in culture: "Black life and black families in America must be understood in the light of broad historical, cultural, social, economic, and political forces that are shaping American society."[50]

"Systems" thinking has become more common in ministry practice today—for example, it is an important emphasis of many publications of the Alban Institute.[51] Systems thinking assumes that problems arise in the interactions between and among people; hence, the entire system must be examined in order to know how to solve issues. However, systems approaches to ministry often focus on the local parish *as* the system. If Smith is to be taken seriously, however, the local parish is not the whole system. Rather, the parish is deeply shaped by larger cultural and social trends. Thus, for Smith, it is the interaction between the workings of the larger society and the daily struggles of church people that must be the focus of good ministry and pastoral care.[52] Therapy, he argues, includes healing at a number of levels, societal as well as individual. Good spiritual care therefore requires attention to multiple levels of suffering, including those large social and cultural images that so often shape our understanding and equally as often are forgotten by the mainstream. "Ignored is the fact that the dominant white culture's misinformed and negative view of African Americans *is* being taught, minds *are* being shaped, and the status quo goes unchallenged. Ideas about white superiority and black inferiority become institutionalized."[53]

Although Smith speaks primarily to and about the black church, we read in his words a very significant challenge to spiritual care for *all* pastors in *all* churches: good spiritual care demands that we not ignore the cultural myths, stereotypes, and prejudices that perpetuate racism and other forms of oppression in our society. Good spiritual care of congregations does not happen simply by attending to *personal* issues presented in individual pastoral counseling or to *institutional* issues presented by the local congregation; it demands a larger *social critique* that focuses on societal levels of injustice that cause suffering for many and distort the perspectives and lives of all.

This larger perspective was almost never reflected in responses from mainstream clergy with whom we spoke, nor does it permeate the literature from the Alban Institute that is otherwise so helpful. Clergy appear to consign spirituality to one or two components of the grid (see chapter 1), ignoring the institutional and larger social dimensions of spiritual life. Further, when they do see institutional dimensions, most clergy think *within* church structures. The best of spiritual care, however, will step *outside* those structures to challenge the presuppositions on which the church itself operates. We are reminded here of Chopp's challenge that it may be the church itself that is most in need of liberation. Pastors who want to do good spiritual care will have to examine their own institutions as well as their cultural settings.

The Ethics of Neglect

What we have been identifying here is the possibility of a category of unethical professional conduct that is not necessarily "spiritual abuse" but may nonetheless raise serious ethical questions: the category of *neglect.*

Neglect involves a failure to assist or to help someone to thrive spiritually. Neglect thus violates the ethical mandate to do good, the mandate of "beneficence" that is incorporated as part of the traditional code of ethics for professionals. However, beneficence is a somewhat problematic requirement. Generally speaking, philosophers have considered the ethical mandate to do good to be less stringent than the mandate to avoid harm. Kant considered avoiding harm a "perfect" obligation—always mandatory—while doing good was an "imperfect" obligation that applied with less rigor. W. D. Ross also placed not-harming as among the most stringent of the "prima facie duties" that guide ethical behavior. Thus, for most people, avoiding harm is a more stringent duty than is doing good. Oppressed groups would remind others as well that they do not need to be "helped" as much as they need not to be harmed. If neglect is simply a failure to do good, should it loom large as an ethical failure?

First, we need to say that neglect of spiritual dimensions

can indeed do harm. While we will turn to the specific question of abuse in chapter 6, we believe that there are circumstances in which neglect is decidedly harmful. Neglect of political dimensions of spirituality such as cultural myths and images that contribute to racism does indeed do harm both to victims of racism and to racists. Both are dehumanized. Neglect of feminist dimensions of spirituality harms all of us either by making it difficult for us to have a relationship with God at all, or by presenting to us a false god for our relating. In Christian understanding, depriving someone of a relationship with God or giving them a false god instead of the true God does significant harm to their spirituality. In short, neglect is not *simply* a matter of failing to do good; it can also be a matter of harming.

But even where neglect is nothing more than a failure to do good, spiritual neglect cuts at the core of clergy responsibilities. Part of the charge to clergy is the spiritual growth and well-being of churches and parishioners. To the extent that this growth and well-being is neglected, clergy are not providing good spiritual care, and are not undertaking a central mandate of their calling. Spiritual neglect is therefore a serious matter for clergy.

We confess to some discomfort at saying this. We are keenly aware of how hard most clergy work, and of how demanding and difficult is the task set before them every day. With the pressure of dwindling resources, the demands of aging congregations, and the strictures brought about by the routines of the workweek, it is possible that clergy are too overwhelmed to step back and look at this "big picture." We acknowledge this, and our hearts go out to colleagues who feel utterly drained and pulled in too many directions at once. We also know that many mainline Protestant denominations have offered little denominational structural support for raising issues related to spirituality. Indeed, sometimes, they have been hostile to clergy who try to address social dimensions of spirituality. Clergy can be caught between a rock and a hard place in their efforts.

Nonetheless, good spiritual care does require an effort to see the big picture and to ask whether spirituality itself is being neglected, or whether spiritual practices that dominate the church are themselves stultifying and failing to bring people's spirituality into contact with all the important dimensions. If spiritual care is "bringing into the light some piece of truth that has not yet been surfaced and confronted and dealt with,"[54] then spiritual care requires that we cast a wide net for truth.

In chapter 1 we proposed a guideline for good spiritual care that requires attention to a fourfold "grid." This grid prevents practitioners from seeing spirituality as only the "interior life."[55] It demands attention to structures and to the environment at large as arenas important to spirituality. Here, we extend that guideline to propose that clergy who deal only with intrapersonal or interpersonal dimensions of their parishioners' spirituality are in fact engaging in spiritual neglect, and that this constitutes an ethical failure. Attending to structures such as family and economic systems is an important part of spiritual care. So, too, is attending to the cultural myths and symbols that shape us. Myths and symbols can make us into caring and compassionate beings capable of empathy with others, or they can shape us into white supremacists or "masculinists" who neglect fundamental issues of social justice. It is for this reason that feminist spirituality stresses the importance of inclusive language: language sets the tone for what we can expect for ourselves and others. Where our language for God is limited and stultifying, so, too, will our spirituality be limited and deadened. Hence, there is a political dimension to spirituality that we neglect at our peril.

Good spiritual care, then, is not simply a matter of responding to the immediate needs or issues brought by parishioners. It is indeed difficult to determine when someone should be asked to leave the church. It is indeed hard to deal with the destruction that those with mental illness can wreak on a congregation. These are crucial issues. But they alone do not fill the well of true spiritual care. The well must be dug deep and include openness to emerging forms of spirituality such as feminist spirituality. It must be filled with the living water of social justice and of a deep and abiding relationship with God. True spiritual care will refuse to ignore the Holocaust or our own painful history of slavery, broken treaties, and oppression of nonwhite peoples. True spiritual care will be social and political as well as personal. Wider issues are not incidental to spiritual care in ministry. They are at the core of spiritual work in congregational settings. Clergy who are making every effort to attend to them deserve our gratitude and support.

In the Introduction, we presented the case of Albert Woodman, who was called to a congregation of older people. They grumbled when he spent his time building a neighborhood watch program and an after-school program for teens. We would argue, however, that doing these things was part of providing good spiritual leadership for his congregation. Albert was attending to the grid and trying to extend an understanding of spirituality beyond the intrapersonal and interpersonal. Similarly, here we would argue that Mark Palmer is not being spiritually abusive when he preaches about "sin." Indeed, we would argue that a failure to lift up social justice issues might be, as suggested by Archie Smith and others, a form of spiritual neglect. Mark Palmer is providing good spiritual care when he asks his parishioners to address all four aspects of the "grid" of spirituality.

CHAPTER 5

Spiritual Care in Specialized and Workplace Ministries

Hospital chaplains, campus ministers, and military chaplains provide ministerial services in settings where religious concerns are understood as related but peripheral to the primary task of the institution in which they serve. These specialized ministry settings, however, offer many opportunities for addressing spiritual issues arising from the lived experience of faith. Questions of life's deepest meaning and significance frequently arise when people are confronting illness, death, crises, or war. Although the educational context is generally less dramatic than is the hospital or military setting, questions of meaning and purpose emerge as students confront the developmental tasks regarding self and life choices, are questioned about their presuppositions, and challenged about their assumptive worldviews. The religious professionals who serve in these ministries do so in the name of and on behalf of the wider church. These professional clergypersons, because of the nature and context of their ministries, require special consideration when exploring the ethical nature of spiritual care.

In this chapter we will explore ethical issues related to the spiritual care provided by specialized and workplace ministries. We will look at the significance of the professional model of ethics as it relates to the work of campus ministers and hospital and military chaplains. Special attention will be devoted to the moral implications of discerning God's transforming activity at the structural level of the grid. We begin with a case study to make tangible the importance and nature of these issues.

A Case: The Anatomy Class

It was a warm summer afternoon when Ted Layton, a professor of anatomy from the medical school, came to the Campus Ministry Office to discuss some of his concerns about students in the anatomy course. Over the years he had noticed two trends that concerned him. First, some students were extremely reluctant to dissect their cadaver. The students usually worked in teams of two or three, and Ted observed that some students seemed to leave the actual dissection to their peers. Another group readily took their scalpels and began work immediately, seemingly delighting in their task. Those in the latter group, however, soon began throwing various organs at one another while engaging in loud, embarrassed laughter as they worked. Obviously both groups were uncomfortable with the task of cutting apart a dead human body as a means to learning the anatomy of human beings. Layton wondered if the campus minister, Maria Elias, had any ideas about how this might be addressed.

To address these issues, Ted and Maria devised a rather comprehensive plan that resulted in changes to the established protocols. Consequently, the medical faculty as a whole needed to approve the plan. For a number of years each spring the medical school had buried the cremated remains of its cadavers at a brief graveside service led by a local Protestant pastor. Family members of those being buried were invited to attend and many did. Ted and Maria developed the idea of inviting the students who would be in the anatomy class the following fall to the spring burial service. Although attendance would not be required, it would be strongly encouraged. The university campus minister would be asked to lead the service and in the course of the event acknowledge that students were attending who would benefit from the gift of the cadavers as an integral aspect of their medical training. Thus, before entering the class, the students would see the families of the cadavers used the previous year. Ted and Maria believed this would give them a sense that the bodies on which they were working had been wives, husbands, friends, and family members to others. The hope was that this would give the students a sense of respect for the cadavers on which they would work, knowing that next spring their cadavers would also be buried in a service at which their families would be present.

Step two of the plan involved the campus minister going into the anatomy lab to lead a short service, which would (1) give thanks for the people who had donated their bodies as gifts to the School of Medicine; (2) acknowledge the anxiety that the students would likely feel when being asked to dissect a body for the first time; (3) affirm the importance of the learning that would be gained through the process for service to those living and in need of competent medical care. Much of the service consisted of a responsive reading involving the campus minister, professors of anatomy, and students.

The medical faculty approved the proposal for a one-year trial period, and Ted and Maria implemented their design. The initial problems with anxiety in the laboratory were greatly reduced, the students treated the bodies with respect, and a number of students decided to attend the burial service at the end of the year to pay their final respects to those whose gifts had aided them in their medical training. The one-year trial period was considered a success and the arrangement continued.

Structures and Spiritual Care

The anatomy class case study provides a number of insights into the structural and organizational implications of spiritual care. It also raises the ethical concerns that are attendant when structural change occurs. Here we explore a few of those issues and consider their implications for other specialized ministries.

First is that the campus minister could have suggested that the professor refer students to her who were anxious about dissecting their cadavers. This approach would have been a traditional one-to-one method for addressing the issue. We see immediately, however, how ineffective such an approach is likely to be. The professor would likely not know ahead of time who was especially anxious, but most of the students would have at least some anxiety facing the dissection of a human body. Were he to announce the campus minister's availability, it is also likely that only a small number of students would respond to the opportunity to talk about the experience.

The decision to treat this as a structural issue for spiritual discernment rather than as a one-to-one pastoral care issue reflects important ethical choices. The campus minister in this situation looked for how God's transforming love might be addressed not simply as individual concern, but through the structures of the educational institution. This required discerning God's activity at each step of the evolving process. Maria and Ted reflected on Ted's hopes as he made the initial decision to approach the campus minister. They listened for the leading of the Spirit in conversation as they worked on a plan and as they developed an approach to the Medical Faculty. Last, they evaluated the impact of these structural changes in the lives of the students and family who were the focus of the interventions. In this circumstance the structural responses to the issues made it possible to create a human community from the various participants (students, faculty, family members of the persons who donated their bodies) even if for only a brief time. This community was able to affirm the sacred nature of human life both in the funeral service for the remains and in the anatomy laboratory. Here the spirit that animates all of life was celebrated and both the living and the dead shared this bond. In addition, the services affirmed the significance of life and provided an affirmation of the gift the students had been bequeathed by the persons who donated their bodies.

The Professional Model of Ethics

In chapter 2 we presented a professional model of ethics and explored the ways in which that model both helpfully informs and yet is ultimately inadequate to addressing a number of the theological and spiritual issues of our time. In this chapter on specialized ministries, we return to the professional model of ethics and find that many of its characteristics are useful in exploring professional issues in many specialized ministries.

Persons in specialized ministries usually have specialized skills and knowledge. This knowledge will at least include the ability to offer ministry in a context other than the traditional congregation. For example, campus ministers need a knowledge of their educational setting (university, college, or junior college; public or private institution). Military chaplains need to understand the highly structured, hierarchical context in which they work, while hospital chaplains must know the nature of the hospital or facility (general, psychiatric, retirement, chronic care) in which they serve. Church administrators who work in regional or national offices also participate in a work environment that often has much in common with other secular institutions.

Those serving in educational, hospital, and military settings will often find themselves ministering to persons whose denominations or faith traditions are not their own. In such circumstances the religious professional will not be expected to be "an expert" on all the denominational and faith stances of those seeking counsel. The ethics of spiritual care, however, requires at least two characteristics of such religious professionals: (1) a willingness to be flexible enough to attempt to see the "issues" from the vantage point of the person seeking assistance; (2) a sense of integrity, which allows the religious professional to share his or her beliefs without claiming that they are the *only* right theological or faith stance. Some general knowledge of other denominations and faiths and a sense of humility about one's own faith tradition can be useful to religious professionals serving diverse populations. In an age of diversity and plurality, the ability of religious professionals to speak about—or, more important, listen to—life's deepest truths from the perspective of more than one symbol system is a precious asset.

Those serving in specialized ministries must also recognize that some people in the organizations they serve may be indifferent or even hostile to them as representatives of the religious community. When one sees the prejudicial attitudes and injustices fostered by some religious groups, it is little wonder that some very caring, committed persons will be hostile to religious issues and religious professionals. Recognizing the difference between indifference and hostility can have strong implications for advocating structural change. Many persons serving in specialized ministries find that people within the institutional structure who are indifferent to religion may nevertheless be advocates for programs and approaches that they understand to benefit the client population. Understanding the nature of the complex organizations in which specialized ministries are performed requires specialized knowledge of the setting, including the context, the employees, and the populations being served. Such knowledge frequently has a direct impact on the spiritual care that is provided to individuals and to the organizational structure per se.

Another characteristic of the professional model of ethics is professional autonomy. Such autonomy is commonplace in most specialized ministries. The campus minister, hospital chaplain, military chaplain, or church administrator is normally accountable to some degree to both the church and to the institution in which he or she serves. The nature of this accountability varies with the ministry, institution, and setting. Typically, however, a clergyperson serving as chaplain, campus minister, or church administrator has a great deal of freedom in setting priorities, managing time, and experimenting with creative or new forms of ministry within the context of the institutional structure. In specialized ministries the chaplain or campus minister is viewed not as a leader of a community of faith but as an individual person in some sense working "alone." It is the religious professional as *person* or in some settings the *office* of the religious professional that symbolically represents the ministry rather than the church or congregation. This contributes to the increased autonomy of those in specialized ministries.

At the same time, there are other contexts where autonomy is hard to come by. In a highly structured, hierarchical setting such as military chaplaincy, for example, clergy may have to obtain approval from their military superiors before being able to act. This creates enormous tension for some, and many brave military chaplains have put their careers on the line on occasion by standing up to superior officers in the name of their faith convictions. In other settings, clergy may be functioning not *as clergy* or as chaplains, but simply as employees of an organization. For example, one clergywoman wrote to us that she is employed by a government agency managing housing for the elderly. Although she sees herself clearly as a clergywoman whose efforts to create fair housing constitute an important form of ministry in the world, she is not employed by a denomination. She is an employee of the agency for which she works, and must abide by its rules and regulations. Thus she has relatively little autonomy in her work.

Turning to goals as delimited in the professional model of ethics, the distinctive goal of specialized ministries depends upon the context in which the ministry is provided. For example, in campus ministry there is an attempt to provide worship, pastoral care, prophetic critique, and social action in the service of justice for students, staff, administrators, and faculty. The form this ministry takes depends upon the type of school, the academic programs offered, and the needs of people within the institution. Military chaplains often provide worship, pastoral care, and a certain degree of advocacy within the military structures to which they are also accountable. Hospital chaplains usually serve on hospital committees where their expertise is sought, do crisis intervention with individuals and families, provide worship opportunities, and through their office facilitate connections between parish clergy and their hospitalized parishioners. The changing nature of medical care—for example, increased outpatient services and shorter hospital visits—and the rise of technological skills that raise ethical issues related to death, dying, and genetics mean that chaplains are often asked to serve families where their life experiences and choices are raising fundamental spiritual questions about life's meaning and the nature of God. These chaplains help persons cope with these issues not as abstract ethical dilemmas but as flesh-and-blood concerns.

Power, Confidentiality, and Discretion

The professional ethics model proscribes the motivation of personal gain and defines the fiduciary relationship toward those one serves. The issues of power and maintaining appropriate boundaries are as germane to specialized ministries as they are to congregational ministries. In many instances the power differential is more pronounced in specialized ministries where pastoral care is provided than in congregational settings. Students, patients, and military persons of lower rank find the campus minister or chaplain in a position with more power than they have. University and hospital administrators as well as high-ranking officers, however, will have considerably more power than the campus minister, hospital chaplain, or military chaplain. Providing spiritual care to those with differing degrees of power requires maintaining appropriate boundaries.

One implication of this for clergy serving in these settings is maintaining strict confidentiality, often treating as confidential information shared in settings that are not typically associated with requirements for confidentiality. The campus minister, or hospital or military chaplain typically associates with persons of diverse power. An effective clergyperson in these settings will frequently gain the confidence of those with whom she or he associates. This ability to cross social, power, class, and rank boundaries will often place the clergyperson in a privileged position of knowing information that will affect those at other levels. Information learned in these often social or casual exchanges must often be treated with great discretion or those who have shared the information may be hurt. In complex organizations the religious professional may well not be privy to information available to those with greater institutional authority. As a result, unforeseen negative consequences may attend inappropriate disclosures by a religious professional about persons at other levels in the organization.

On the positive side, the clergyperson's position may make him or her a useful negotiator and helpful advocate for those with less power if the position is used with faithfulness and integrity. However, self-insight and care are required here, too. An obvious danger is the clergyperson who wants to "do good" or "help others" without a sense of appropriate personal and role boundaries. Such persons frequently wonder why their attempts to seek more just conditions for those in need have contributed to further harm. Ill-timed or ill-conceived interventions often result in the marginalization of the clergyperson and the devaluing of that which he or she has advocated.

Another danger emerges if the campus minister, or hospital or military chaplain simply becomes the instrument of the employing institution. Here the prophetic edge can be lost. Institutional policies that diminish the human spirit need to be challenged by the light of the gospel. Clergy should lead and support critiques of institutions that diminish persons because of their gender, sexual orientation, class, or race. The complex organizations in which clergy in specialized ministries work are as likely to need this critique as is the institutional church.

Recognizing Specialized and Workplace Ministries

Those who work in specialized ministries often report that they feel the institutional church does not sufficiently claim or value their ministry. This lack of concern for the work of those in specialized settings may be expressed in a number of ways. As budgets have shrunk over the past decade, often specialized ministries are the first to receive funding cuts. It is also true that those who work in more traditional ministerial settings frequently expect clergy in specialized ministries to be as fully involved in congregational life as a full-time parish pastor. While those within the institutional church structure may feel those in specialized ministries are not sufficiently interested in institutional activities, it is also true that specialized ministries are often viewed as "not fully ministry." Numerous campus ministers and hospital chaplains report that persons within the congregational structure will ask them if they "plan to come back into ministry" someday! Such questions reveal an insensitivity to the crucial spiritual dimensions that persons in specialized ministries address, both in their ministries with individuals and with the institutional structures themselves.

As the lives of increasing numbers of people are shaped by urban, institutional cultures it seems especially important to claim creative attempts to minister to people in their workplace. When we think of the number of small congregations who claim the resources of a full-time pastor, it seems as though it might be more faithful to continue to explore ministry settings that provide pastoral services where people live so much of their lives—namely, the workplace. As the financial resources of the institutional church shrink, competing demands for resources seem destined to truncate much of the creative work of specialized ministries, especially new ventures.

Workplace Spirituality

Workplace spirituality is gaining increased attention as both business schools and programs in spiritual direction take seriously the structural aspects of spiritual care. In the business world these concerns are often the focus of attention for corporate coaches who help employers and employees explore their value systems and the values being embodied in the products of corporations as well as the output of employees. A supplement in the *Los Angeles Times* called "The Soul At Work"[1] calls attention to the current interest in workplace spirituality. The titles of articles by staff journalists suggest something of the nature of the interest: "A Profession of Faith: More and more people want spirituality in their jobs—but what does that mean?"; "Higher Power Lunches: An increasing number of businesses are letting employees hold on-site religious study sessions"; "The Missing Link: For many work lost its spiritual dimension. . . . Now baby boomers are seeking to bring back soul"; "Amen at the Top: One boss prays for the company and his employees."

This attention to spirituality in the workplace results in at least three types of literature. First, there are articles and books dealing with spiritual practices in which individuals can engage while in their work setting.[2] With this material the focus is on the individual and small groups. Ethical issues become significant. The use of individual spiritual practices may help an individual employee grow and deepen both personally and professionally.

Such practices, however, can also serve only to help people cope with situations that require more radical transformation. For example, when an employee is having difficulty with a coworker, it may be that there are psychological and spiritual issues occurring in the person's life that require further work. In such cases the conflict is an opportunity for growth and transformation if viewed from that perspective. In other circumstances spiritual practices can be used to deny or avoid a problem that needs to be faced. Some people writing about the workplace suggest such things as the importance of whistling a happy tune as a spiritual practice for dealing with difficult circumstances. Although we can affirm whistling on given occasions, the ethical concern here is that situations that require analysis, critique, and behavior change either by individuals or the corporate structure may be made to seem trivial by such an approach and remain unaddressed. If spiritual practices are used to help people endure situations that should be transformed, the spiritual practice is simply a coping technique in the service of harmony or productivity. Individual and small group Bible study or prayer groups, for example, can be significant avenues to spiritual growth, but they must also be subject to analysis and evaluation or risk becoming only a coping technique. Such groups when functioning well may sustain those who need support when raising crucial moral issues in the corporate board rooms and offices. In our pluralistic society, groups may also form around values concerns where a variety of approaches and faiths are welcome. Such groups can provide support without mandating any given doctrine or ideology.

A second body of literature explores the spiritual dimensions of the corporate culture.[3] Here the structural level of discernment on the grid is taken seriously. This literature integrates ethical and moral concerns into the process of discerning where God's transforming love is at work in the structure. This analysis can center on the company's product, with such questions as: What is the value of the product? What need does it meet in the society? Is the need a genuine human need or an artificial need created primarily through advertising? Corporate coaches can also help business executives explore the culture of the workplace: What is valued in a trusted employee? What work patterns are being encouraged? How does the work environment contribute to employee well-being? This approach to discernment raises the ethical issues created by the value systems of those who shape company policy and define the office environment. It takes seriously the reality that God's transforming love is at work in the world. The issue for workplace spirituality is to discern where God is already moving in the company and to work to enhance this movement.

Third, a number of books and articles relevant to workplace spirituality provide an analysis and critique of the wider economic and corporate cultures in global markets.[4] These works explore the nature of work itself; they are not interested in spiritual discernment per se, but their analytical stance exposes the culture that undergirds and shapes much of the broader economic and political environment. These studies explore how work functions in our society and help us see that "getting a job" is not merely a matter of personal responsibility.

If the tendency to overlook specialized ministries within the church is common, the failure of the institutional church to recognize and claim the ministry of its members in the workplace is endemic. Robert Wuthnow notes that clergy and religious professionals have failed to connect spirituality with the workplace.[5] Clergy, especially those influenced by Reformed theology, speak of people's work as a vocation. Too often, however, this has been interpreted as finding the job that "makes you feel good." In the San Francisco area we hear radio advertisements that speak of "following your bliss."[6] By "following your bliss" it is assumed that you will end up with a job where satisfaction will be its own reward. Yet when one looks at the job opportunities, it is clear that choice is not nearly so abundant as the advertisements suggest. Such approaches tend to blame the unemployed individual if work is not found, when in reality the economic system may not be providing sufficient offerings.

Within the parish structure we have little understanding of this economic reality. There is also scant evidence that the spiritual implications of the theological notion of vocation are used to critique the notion of "follow your bliss." A true vocation may contribute to the good of the society yet may not be especially blissful. For followers of Christ it may at times mean taking up a cross and walking on when the going is difficult.

In general the church has been slow to understand the spiritual implications of work and the workplace. The workplace today has at least four crucial characteristics: First, people are under constant time pressure as the demands for increased productivity escalate. Currently people are asked to work, on average, one hundred fifty more hours a year than they were in 1910.[7] Second, middle-class persons, who make up the great majority of congregations, are often in positions where the demands of decision making regarding persons, programs, and products are intense.[8] The decisions frequently involve both economic and human resources and are especially difficult during times of mergers and downsizing when people often find their positions eliminated. Third, job stress is very high because of both the increased demands and the issues requiring resolution. Fourth, unemployment is not uncommon for persons who have been employed for many years in positions they deemed secure.[9]

Given this situation, what are people finding as they turn to religious professionals for guidance? Unfortunately what they often find is a church culture that has not taken seriously the changed realities of the workplace. Instead of sustained ethical reflection on the nature of work and its importance for the human spirit, many religious communities continue to extol the clichéd platitudes about the virtue of "hard work." Wuthnow's research revealed that many sermons reinforce the value of working hard as an aspect of faithfulness to God, without any awareness that the demands of the workplace are becoming unrealistic and destructive to the human spirit. Further, church members

120

are encouraged to make their families a priority at the same time they are told to "work hard," with little awareness that in contemporary urban culture the two values may well be in conflict. People may need to make choices about how hard they work and how much time they spend with their families. Women have been in the middle of this double bind for some time as they are expected—both by others and by themselves—to provide for a household physically and emotionally as well as bring home a paycheck needed to meet the monthly bills. The feminist critique should help us recognize that we need to continue examining the demands of this workplace, rather than ignoring it. Wuthnow found one local church where the church leaders said they did not support working mothers—so they provided no day-care options. In that particular congregation, 70 percent of the women in the church worked![10] In another church Wuthnow found that four men had committed suicide after the loss of their jobs. In these cases the sense of personal failure was not alleviated by their religious communities, which failed to understand the ethical issues raised by the contemporary workplace.

This failure on the part of the church to incorporate an adequate critique of the workplace or a vision of the appropriate role of work in the contemporary world has resulted in a parish culture that continues to extol uncritically the value of "hard work." Thus in a workplace where people are under increased pressure to be increasingly productive there is little congregational support for those who are victims of the system. In fact, we have seen that parish attitudes often contribute to the time-bind of their members by instilling a sense of guilt in those who are unable or unwilling to devote hours of volunteer service to congregational concerns.

Conclusion

It is difficult to establish general norms for specialized ministries, as the requirements of each ministry setting must be taken into account when determining how to provide ethical spiritual care. Nonetheless, several crucial components stand out.

First, in many specialized ministries, the power of the clergyperson is magnified because of lack of institutional accountability to the wider church. Power gaps are morally relevant, and they bring to bear the requirements of the traditional model of professional ethics, with its fiduciary demands and its need for clarity about boundaries. Thus, in settings where clergy have great freedom to act, and move within circles of different power, we suggest that boundaries must be drawn with care and that confidentiality must be kept.

Second, clergy who serve in specialized ministries have a particular duty and opportunity to lift up the structural aspects of their settings. A university chaplain should not be content simply to provide care to those who come into the office seeking assistance; rather, her or his role is precisely to look at the institution as a whole and to ask where in the institution spiritual care is needed. On occasion, as in our example of Maria Elias, this means changing structures within the institution so that spiritual needs are met more broadly than a one-on-one setting can provide.

Third, clergy in specialized ministries also have a particular duty and opportunity to move beyond the limits of their own denominational settings and to recognize the Spirit in everyone. "Bad practice" here might mean, as one of our respondents put it, "enforcing conformity" or trying to make others conform to a particular doctrine, interpretation of Scripture, or faith perspective. Because those in specialized ministries must deal with seekers who come out of different faith traditions—or out of no tradition at all—it is incumbent upon them to attempt to help those seekers find their own spiritual resources. Specialized ministries often have a deep and powerful impact on seekers. We know of many clergy who were first influenced to enter ministry by the witness of a college chaplain. Precisely because of the depth and power their impact can have, ethical practice requires an attempt to keep open a breadth of possibilities for the seeker. A crucial requirement is staying open to the uniqueness of each individual, not "type casting" them on the basis of long experience.

Finally, we have suggested that the workplace looms large in the lives of most Americans. Although all clergy have a responsibility to recognize and respond to the spiritual needs associated with work in the contemporary context, there may also be a structural need for churches and denominations to consider specialized ministries in workplaces or specialized ministries that focus on the workplace.

Whether as spiritual directors, as parish pastors, or in specialized ministry settings, clergy confront difficult ethical issues in providing adequate and ethical spiritual care. When may they confront those in their charge? When should they challenge institutions and when should they focus on individual needs and issues? How should they incorporate feminist perspectives when churches are still sexist and reluctant to utilize new images for God or Spirit? How can they assist middle-class church members to see money as a spiritual matter, and how can they simultaneously keep a focus on issues that go beyond the immediate needs of the middle class to remember the emancipatory proclamation of the gospel and its implicit spiritual demands? The tasks that confront ministers in all these situations are not easy to resolve, and it is no wonder that differences arise, leading to charges of neglect or abuse. We have addressed problems of neglect (see chapter 4), and we now turn to sort out some difficult allegations of spiritual abuse.

PART THREE

SPIRITUAL ABUSE

CHAPTER 6

Spiritual Abuse

In October 1895, Frank Sandford founded the Holy Ghost and Us Bible School, the beginnings of a movement that became known as Shiloh. Sandford was the only teacher, and his interpretation was law. Believing strongly that God spoke directly to him, he demanded that his followers see his edicts as having divine sanction. Every aspect of their lives came under his scrutiny, including sex and marriage. Obedience to his will was "nonnegotiable and absolute." To question his authority was to bring disharmony to the group—a sin resulting in severe reprimand. Followers later told stories of harsh punishment for any infractions. One woman said she was "metaphysically stoned"—made to lie on the floor while other members circled her screaming curses at her "spiritual lapses." Intimidation was routine; freedom was unknown. Suffering was to be endured as a sign of blessing. Even small children were beaten or starved when they disobeyed.[1]

Shiloh is a late-nineteenth-century example of a religious

group constituted by the authoritarian leadership of a charismatic personality. Such religious groups—often pejoratively referred to as cults—continue to stir debate because of the harsh and authoritarian demands required of their followers. Such groups make us acutely aware that where there is good spiritual care, there can also be bad spiritual care, failures of care, and even outrageous practices.

When do such failures or practices constitute "abuse"? One woman said that she felt "battered" by the institutional church because of its neglect of feminist issues.[2] Another stays in the church, but says that the "beating" she takes there is "taking its toll."[3] Where parishioners experience church as "battering" or "beating" them, does this constitute a form of spiritual abuse? In chapter 4 we raised the question whether clergy who neglect important aspects of spirituality are simply failing to do good or whether they are actually abusing parishioners. In this chapter, we return to this difficult question, to see if we can define abuse and locate its salient ethical features.

The term "spiritual abuse" seems to be a rather new one, but it is gaining currency.[4] Lloyd Rediger uses it in describing the "killing" actions of parishioners toward clergy.[5] Archie Smith, Jr., uses it in describing why some gay and lesbian people leave the church.[6] Michael Langone uses it in talking about recovery from cults.[7] Flora Wuellner uses it to describe spiritual practices that focus on the structures of religion rather than on our freedom in relationship with the divine.[8] The Linns use it in describing their own spiritual journeys and recovery from certain church practices and experiences.[9]

But above all, two books brought the term to public attention. One of these is Enroth's *Churches That Abuse*, from which the story of Shiloh is taken. The second is David Johnson and Jeff VanVonderen's *Subtle Power of Spiritual Abuse*.[10] Both of these texts argue explicitly that spiritual abuse happens in ministry settings, that it is a violation of true Christian principles, and that it can and should be overcome. It was Johnson and VanVonderen's book that led church officials and their attorneys to bring to Karen Lebacqz the request for an expert witness on "spiritual abuse." It was the subsequent struggle with this book that led Karen to invite Joe Driskill into the extended study that has resulted in the volume at hand.

"Abuse" is a strong term. Dictionary definitions range from "mistreatment" to "corrupt practice,"[11] but in general the term "abuse" is meant to raise strong negative reactions. There are ethical issues in the choice of terminology itself. Does the term "abuse" merely sensationalize? Does it help us to formulate an ethical perspective on providing spiritual care? What is meant by "spiritual abuse"? When should this term be applied? These are the questions to be addressed in this chapter.

As might be expected, not everyone using the term "spiritual abuse" means the same thing by it. We will review the literature briefly, raising some concerns and questions about the varying uses of this provocative term. This discussion will set the stage for our analysis of the ethical anatomy of abuse compared with incompetence or other forms of bad spiritual care. We will explore the spiritual abuse of parishioners by clergy and of clergy by parishioners.

"Spiritual Abuse" of Parishioners

Enroth

Ronald Enroth's *Churches That Abuse* provides profiles of a number of churches based on testimony and interviews with former members who consider their experiences abusive. While Enroth makes every effort to allow their stories to stand as told to him, he draws from those stories a composite picture of spiritual abuse.[12]

The spiritually abusive church is characterized first and foremost by strong, control-oriented leadership.[13] Control extends to every aspect of life—spiritual, physical, and relational. Followers are often told where they may live, what jobs they may have, whom they may marry, what they may eat, and even with whom they may speak. As was the case at Shiloh, dissent is discouraged. Indeed, any questioning of the leader's authority is taken to be a sign of sin. Thus, raising questions will result in being told that one is out of favor with God and needs to repent or be corrected. Correction itself is strict, even painful. Tactics such as public humiliation, separation from families, even physical abuse are not uncommon. Members are often drawn in by promises of love and community, only to find themselves subjected to extreme peer pressure and public scoldings. Complete dependency on the church is fostered by ensuring that no friends or family from "outside" are allowed. The church itself is seen as having the only "true" understanding and being above criticism. Breaking people's spirits is understood to be important in order to help them get closer to God.

Enroth concludes that abusive churches are characterized by a perversion of power on the part of the leader, disruption of families and other healthy relationships, unhealthy dependence of members on leaders, and spiritual confusion in people's lives.[14] Since the word of the leader is equated with God's word, to go against the leader or be forced out of the church is seen as being separated from Jesus. For a serious Christian, this is the ultimate punishment. Thus, it is very difficult for members to leave such churches. Enroth argues that the effects of spiritual abuse are similar to those experienced by rape victims or those of post–traumatic stress syndrome of war veterans; it often takes years to recover. Perhaps most sobering, Enroth reminds us that spiritual abuse can take place in the context of doctrinally sound and biblically based Christianity. The key ingredient is a pastor accountable to no one and therefore beyond confrontation.

Johnson and VanVonderen

While Enroth largely tells stories of abusive churches, Johnson and VanVonderen make an effort to define spiritual abuse. In *The Subtle Power of Spiritual Abuse,* they propose that "spiritual abuse occurs when someone is treated in a way that damages them spiritually."[15] This initial picture equates abuse with damage, but it leaves the reader wanting to know what constitutes spiritual "damage." Johnson and VanVonderen clarify this in their formal definition:

> Spiritual abuse is the mistreatment of a person who is in need of help, support, or greater spiritual empowerment, with the result of weakening, undermining, or decreasing that person's spiritual empowerment.[16]

Based on this definition, spiritual abuse would appear to occur whenever someone's sense of self or connection to God (their "spiritual empowerment") is weakened, undermined, or decreased. Such damage constitutes abuse.

As examples of spiritual abuse, Johnson and VanVonderen offer cases involving shaming or manipulating people,[17] taking away the church as a "safe space,"[18] telling a troubled person that *she* is the problem,[19] presenting a God who increases rather than lifts burdens,[20] and using Scripture as a harsh measuring stick for judging people to be unacceptable to God.[21] These examples suggest that the "damage" envisioned includes both undermining one's sense of self (shaming, making someone believe that *they* are the problem) and undermining one's sense of being loved by and acceptable to God (judging, seeing God as punishing, etc.). Thus, some instances of abuse involve primarily the degradation of *human* spirit, while others specifically target the relationship between human and *divine* Spirit.

Johnson and VanVonderen refine their general definition of spiritual abuse to include at least three typical behaviors:

1. Spiritual abuse happens when a leader uses his or her spiritual position to control or dominate others. Here, they pick up Enroth's emphasis on control.
2. Spiritual abuse happens when leaders require "spiritual

performance" in accord with an exacting standard and then make people feel inadequate when they cannot meet that standard. Here, engendering a sense of unworthiness becomes central to abuse.

3. Spiritual abuse happens when judgment is leveled at someone who is in need of support. Here, abuse centers on shaming.[22]

In most instances, spiritual abuse involves leaving someone feeling that their spirituality is defective; in many instances shame is used to get someone to support the view of the more powerful person.

Based on these examples and definitions, Johnson and VanVonderen propose that there is a certain *anatomy* to spiritual abuse. This anatomy, or structure, includes the fact that one party is powerful and the other more vulnerable or weak, that the powerful one assumes that his or her authority is beyond question, and that the powerful one shifts the focus of concern away from the problem as perceived by the vulnerable one and toward seeing the vulnerable person as the problem.[23] Spiritual abuse, they argue, can only come from a place of power or perceived power.[24] Thus, most of the time, abuse will be perpetrated by the leader or professional who holds power in the situation.[25]

Johnson and VanVonderen's understanding of spiritual abuse is grounded in two roots. First is a scriptural root that defines "false" spiritual leaders (Matthew 23) and compares two spiritual systems (Matt. 11:28-30, and passim). The "true" spiritual system is under the reign of God and intends to bring life and freedom to people. The "false" spiritual system is under the rule of people, who try to control the behavior of others.[26] In a true spiritual system, God's yoke is light (Matt. 11:30). Jesus railed against false spiritual leaders in his day, they propose, and similarly there will be false spiritual leaders in our day. When weary souls go to church, they seek "living water" but are in danger of finding "vipers" who suck their lifeblood instead.[27]

The second root is family systems theory, in which abusive family systems are understood in terms of shame-based relations that undermine one's sense of self. In a healthy family, they suggest, people are allowed to make mistakes, and at root the personhood of the child is affirmed. Parents who create an "unsafe space" by being too harsh and judgmental, or holding up standards that are impossible for children to meet, or tearing their children down, or using their children to meet their *own* needs, are abusive.[28] That they are particularly concerned with shame-based relationships can be seen from the fact that they devote an entire chapter to a discussion of the characteristics of shame-based relationships.[29] Indeed, it appears that much of the literature on spiritual abuse uses family systems as its model, and is particularly concerned with *shame* as abusive.[30] We see this theme emerge again in the work of the Linns.

The Linns

Three people who consider themselves to be "slowly recovering from spiritual abuse" add fuel to the fire. Matthew Linn, Sheila Fabricant Linn, and Dennis Linn all consider spiritual abuse to be closely connected to religious addiction, and both of those phenomena to be rooted in shame-based patterns.

Key to their view is a sense of spiritual *freedom*.[31] They suggest that religious leaders are often caught in addictive patterns in which they have found their own substance or process to use to escape from painful realities; they then try to force others to use the same substance or process "by telling them there is only one way to God, *my* way."[32]

For the Linns, then, spiritual abuse consists largely in efforts to *control* and *limit* or confine another's spiritual path or growth. Basing their model largely on family systems theory, they draw heavily on patterns of *shaming* that leave people disliking themselves.[33] Much of their book is devoted to addressing ways that children learn to deal with being shamed—by rebelling, by trying to be perfect, by getting lost or quietly withdrawing, or by distracting through humor.[34]

The Linns' approach to spiritual abuse appears to focus more heavily on the abuse of children by their parents than on specific practices in churches or by clergy. Indeed, Sheila Fabricant Linn tells her story of coming from a family that could not provide a safe place for her, but learning to be safe in exploring her spirituality later during her studies of religion at the Graduate Theological Union.[35] Thus, the Linns appear to suggest that spiritual abuse may happen in families and that clergy or churches may serve a role in *healing* the spiritual abuse of childhood. Nonetheless, their approach has implications for professional ethics. It suggests that *control* of others' spirituality, rather than opening space for their own growth, is abusive. Under such a definition, a pastor who restricts legitimate spiritual expression to a single model that fits his or her own proclivities would likely be considered to be spiritually abusive. Further, the Linns suggest that spiritual abuse can consist in *neglecting* another's spiritual growth.[36] This has implications for whether the term can be applied to mainstream clergy who neglect dimensions of spirituality, as identified in chapter 4.

Langone and Others

A third volume that uses the explicit phrase "spiritual abuse" is Langone's edited volume *Recovery from Cults*.[37] As the title suggests, here the discussion of spiritual abuse is linked explicitly with new religious groups or offshoots, rather than with mainstream churches or even with family systems. Few of the essays included in this volume discuss spiritual abuse directly. Nonetheless, like the Linns, several authors appear to take their cue from models of addiction and recovery. Tobias suggests that cult experiences are often felt to be a kind of "spiritual rape" or all-consuming addiction from which recovery is necessary. Dowhower proposes that former cult members often lack the spiritual discernment that allows mature people to distinguish which religious truth claims are legitimate and which are not. A number of the authors in this volume see a cult as an all-consuming system that gives meaning and direction to adherents' lives in a way similar to addiction. Although there is little explicit discussion of what would constitute spiritual abuse, the underlying assumption appears to be that such all-consuming systems are abusive of people's spirituality, blocking appropriate growth and development of skills of discernment, and changing even personalities on a very deep level. Here again, then, abuse would appear to consist in limiting spirituality to a particular path or system, in blocking or preventing the growth of skills of spiritual discernment, and in depriving people of a solid sense of self.

We note that the term "cult" is itself a value-laden term, evoking strong negative reactions. For this reason, we understand Enroth's use of "church" even when describing small offshoots that have no denominational affiliations. It is always tempting to assign a value-laden term to that which we do not like, but it is an ethically problematic practice. After all, all churches offer an interpretation of reality and hope that their adherents will come to see the world through their own value system; in this regard, "cults" are no different from mainline "churches." They may be more effective at ensuring that adherents do in fact adopt the desired perspective, but their goals are not necessarily different from those of mainline churches. Those who study religious groups as a phenomenon generally prefer the term "new religious groups."[38]

Rediger

Lloyd Rediger is well known for his work with pastors. In *Clergy Killers,* he looks primarily at circumstances where churches or parishioners abuse clergy (see the discussion that concludes this chapter). Nonetheless, in one chapter, he turns the tables and discusses not clergy killers but "killer

135

clergy" who abuse parishioners. Rediger's model is drawn from a mental health paradigm that assumes that normal conflict is not only acceptable but also can be healthy for a church. "Normal" conflict is the product of diversity in any group. It is subject to rational discussion and caring management. There is also, however, "abnormal" conflict, in which one of the parties has a mental or personality disorder. In such cases, rational discussion will not be useful. The person needs "tough love"—discipline in a context of love and support. Finally, there is "spiritual" conflict, in which one of the parties is deliberately intent upon destruction of self or others. The last category clearly constitutes "abuse" for Rediger. Here, a parishioner or clergyperson lies, manipulates, and aligns himself or herself with evil in order to destroy other people.[39]

"Killer clergy" who spiritually abuse their parishioners are against life and wholeness. They deliberately interfere with the health of a church or its members. Rediger tells the story of a pastor who failed to call on parishioners, demanded to be paid for expenses but refused to produce receipts for those expenses, was never prepared for teaching Bible study classes, and generally failed to carry out his ministerial functions. Three board members had resigned and two had left the church. The pastor's "persistent pattern of destructive behavior" leads Rediger to suggest that this was not simply a matter of incompetence, but of abuse.

A Composite Picture

Taking these works seriously, the picture of *spiritual abuse* of parishioners by clergy would look something like this:

1. Spiritual abuse can consist in
   • *damaging or diminishing* parishioners' spiritual growth;
   • *controlling or confining* parishioners' spiritual growth; or possibly
   • *neglecting* parishioners' spiritual growth;

2. The notion that some spiritual practices can be defined as *abusive* has *scriptural warrants* in the discussions of false spiritual leaders.
3. The understanding of spiritual abuse rejects any perpetrating of *shame* in personal and spiritual development.
4. Spiritual abuse is also seen as closely linked to patterns of *addiction* in which people try to find meaning in an all-consuming system, structure, or process that in fact limits their human freedom and growth or makes them control others.
5. Although spiritual abuse can happen between any two people, it is linked with *power* or perceived power and thus is most likely to be perpetrated by a spiritual leader or director.

Applying and Challenging the Analysis

On the basis of these descriptions, examples, and definitions, it is easy to see why the case originally brought to Karen appeared to be a case of spiritual abuse. The charges against the pastor in this case included constant belittling of parishioners, judging them inadequate rather than supporting them, having rigid standards that they must meet, but, of course, finding that they never met those standards and then berating them for their poor performance, and refusing to allow any questioning of the pastor's judgment or direction. If indeed the minister of this church was constantly belittling his parishioners and leveling judgment at them rather than supporting them, he appears to have been engaging in one of the typical behaviors identified by Johnson and VanVonderen. Similarly, if he refused to allow his authority to be questioned, and insisted on controlling and dominating every spiritual exchange in the parish, he was taking away the church as a safe space and trying to use his spiritual position to control and dominate others. On the surface, his behavior—if it was indeed as alleged—would appear to fit the composite picture of "spiritual abuse." He appeared to control parishioners' spirituality, to damage or diminish their sense of self and relation to God, and to use his power to shame them and strip them of their sense of value in God's eyes. Rather than enhancing their relation to God, many parishioners felt that he moved them farther and farther away from God.

And yet, we are troubled. Is every instance of controlling a parishioner's behavior abusive? Would the minister in this case have been considered abusive if he did not exhibit a *pattern* of controlling behavior, but only occasional *moments* of trying to control? What if he did not *belittle* his parishioners, but simply *neglected* them? Would that be abusive? Each of the authors reviewed in this chapter would appear to put emphasis in a slightly different place in defining abuse, so that some behaviors might be considered spiritual abuse under some definitions, but not under others. For example, the Linns suggest that neglect is a form of spiritual abuse. But their model is drawn from families and early childhood experiences. Neglect of children by their parents may be spiritually abusive, undermining the child's sense of value and worth; but neglect of parishioners by clergy is not necessarily similarly abusive. Much depends on the circumstances.

In the case on which Karen consulted, some spiritual abuse charges involved neglect: it was alleged that the pastor had failed to visit a family in crisis, whose child had recently died. Generally speaking, most churches would expect their pastors to visit those in crisis or grief. Failure to do so might be considered very wrong, possibly even abusive. Yet there were mitigating circumstances: the pastor had suffered his own recent loss, and he was also involved in a very time-consuming legal suit that drained many hours that might otherwise have been spent with parishioners. Was he abusive? Was he simply neglectful? Was he incompetent but not necessarily abusive? Where is the boundary between "abuse" and simple incompetence? Are there times when neglect is wrong but excusable, or simply a matter of incompetence rather than abuse? What makes an action *abusive*?

138

An Ethical Analysis

It seems clear to us that the literature thus far on spiritual abuse draws heavily not only on "fringe" groups but also on experiences of people who have been in very restrictive and demanding church settings such as fundamentalist churches that set strict standards for appropriate expression of spiritual gifts—for example, that one must speak in tongues or that one may not speak at all. For all these authors, the prototypical experience of spiritual abuse is likened to the experience of being shamed as a child—an experience that leaves one confused, scared, and without a secure sense of self. For all these authors, new religious groups, with their rigid requirements and tendency to tear the adherent down, provide a clear instance of abusive spiritual treatment. For all these authors, shame-based systems are considered inherently abusive. Although we might agree that many of the instances they offer do appear to be cases of spiritual abuse, we are nonetheless troubled by the assumptions that appear to underlie these discussions. We believe more clarity is needed, lest allegations of spiritual abuse run amok in the church.

Correction and Judgment

Let us begin with the question of setting standards for spiritual practice and making parishioners feel inadequate if they cannot meet those standards. Setting impossible standards, and then judging and belittling those who fail to meet them, appears to several of our authors (Johnson and VanVonderen, Enroth) to be abusive. Yet it is difficult to know how one would draw a line here. The setting of standards—even very difficult ones—is surely not problematic. Churches that require their members to tithe are setting a standard for acceptable spiritual practice. The standard is demanding and rigid, and may indeed be impossible for some, but it is not alone abusive. Similarly, requiring weekly attendance to sustain membership is a rigid and difficult standard, but hardly abusive in itself. Requiring certain disciplines of prayer may present very real hardships for some members, but again is not abusive per se. All churches set some standards, which those who wish to be members must strive to meet. Having standards cannot alone constitute abuse, or all churches would be guilty of spiritual abuse.

It seems, then, that it is not standards alone, but the response to those who do not meet standards, that constitutes abuse. Yet here, too, we have cautions. Having standards implies that one can be corrected when one fails to meet the standard. As we have seen, Walter Wiest and Elwyn Smith propose precisely that "the pastor has a special (though not exclusive) responsibility to see that the congregation stays on track, to be sure that what it does is consistent with the gospel and is fitting for the body of Christ taking shape in the world."[40] In proposing that the minister has responsibility to see that the congregation stays on track, Wiest and Smith would appear to allow room for the minister to make judgments, and to tell parishioners that they are not serving God appropriately. That is to say, clergy would appear to have a role in *correcting* parishioners' behavior, including their spiritual practices. To be sure, we see no argument in Wiest and Smith for the harsh, judgmental clergy of whom Johnson and VanVonderen or Enroth speak. Nonetheless, if clergy are allowed to keep parishioners on track, there must be room for appropriate correction. When is correction appropriate, and when is it abusive? Is judgment and condemnation of a parishioner necessarily abusive?

Consider the following case. Ed comes to his pastor and confesses that he has had many affairs and is fearful that he will lose his marriage, but he is not ready to give up his latest affair. Hearing this story, the Reverend Stiles suspects that Ed has some deep-seated insecurities. She wants to provide support for him, but she also feels compelled as part of her role as pastor to remind him that adultery is wrong, as it has always been judged to be in the church. Indeed, she tells him that in committing adultery he is sinning against God and against his spouse, and that he must repent and make restitution for his sins. Is this response abusive, because it uses her position of authority to castigate him for his behavior? Or is there a proper role for clergy to tell parishioners that they are wrong, and that their behavior does not serve God's purposes in the world?

Johnson and VanVonderen suggest that spiritual abuse is happening whenever clergy attempt to control or dominate the other, using their spiritual position to do so. How does one reconcile this view that it is wrong for clergy to control the behavior of others with the view that clergy, like other professionals, have a certain kind of authority that is rightly used for the upbuilding of the church and its members, and that such upbuilding may include correcting those who are out of line? We would argue that correcting those who fail to meet standards is not necessarily abusive. Leveling judgment is not an inappropriate part of the pastoral role so long as it is done in love.

Contemporary Christianity often wants to portray God in terms of love, acceptance, openness, and lightness of being. However, the historical record of Christianity includes a judging God who condemns exploitation of the oppressed, rails against those who "trample the heads of the poor," and expects humans to denounce injustice. Indeed, if the broad perspective that we have urged on spirituality is adopted, failure to denounce the Holocaust or slavery or other oppressive practices must be seen as itself potentially spiritually abusive. In other words, there may be circumstances in which a *failure to judge* is abusive! How can we keep room for appropriate judgment, but protect against abusive judgment? What is the distinction between appropriate and abusive judgment?

Shame

We suspect that the real issue for Johnson, VanVonderen, and others is not the presence of standards, or the fact of judgment itself, but the *type* of judgment exercised when standards are not met. Johnson and VanVonderen take issue with clergy who would stand in judgment over the spiritual practices of their parishioners, but their real concern appears to be judgments that belittle or shame the parishioner. For many of the authors writing about new religious movements, and for the Linns in their own spiritual journeys, the abuse appears to lie in judgmental attitudes and statements that shame others. Behavior is considered abusive when it leads to shame or to a diminished sense of self.

We both agree and disagree with this line of reasoning. We agree with a basic assumption that appropriate judgment is "judgment in love." Judgment given in love judges the act, but does not diminish the essential personhood of the actor. As church people sometimes put it, "God hates the sin, but loves the sinner." All of us are sinners. In that regard, when the Reverend Stiles faces Ed, she will recall that he is no more a sinner than she is herself, though their sins may be different. She will also offer him the love and forgiveness of God, if he is truly ready to repent. The "judgment" she levels at his behavior is meant not to destroy him, but to help him get back on track toward being the person God wants him to be. In this sense, then, we agree that he should not leave their meeting with a diminished sense of self.

At the same time, we caution against an automatic rejection of a positive role for shame in Christian life. The Linns define shame as a "toxic, debilitating core sense of being unlovable and inferior as a person."[41] If this is what shame is, then we are inclined to agree that shaming someone is spiritually abusive. Actions that take away one's sense of being lovable or that make a person feel that God could not possibly love that person, are indeed spiritually abusive. We acknowledge that there are circumstances in which shame can have a negative impact on one's spiritual life. Deep and abiding shame that creates a permanent barrier between oneself and others, or between oneself and God, does indeed erode true spirituality. As Nancy Ramsay points out, chronic fear and shame do distort religious experience.[42] To the

142

extent that Johnson and VanVonderen or the Linns have in mind this kind of chronic shame—which appears to be implied by the Linns' definition we have quoted—we concur that engendering such shame harms someone's spirituality. Under these circumstances, engendering shame can be abusive.

However, such chronic, deep, and debilitating shame is not the only form of shame. Shame need not be seen as a core sense of being unlovable. In its more general usage, shame is the feeling engendered when we think that our community does not approve of us or of something we have said or done. We are ashamed when we feel that we cannot hold our heads up high. Such shame is a normal part of almost everyone's experiences of growing up. Shame helps us to keep our behavior and thought patterns in line with our community.

For example, many years ago, I (Karen) turned away a person who came to my door seeking help. Although I tried to direct him to the appropriate community to get help, afterward I felt a deep sense of shame over turning him away. Many times I felt that I had turned Christ away from my door. That sense of shame was a reminder of what God expects of me as a Christian, and of how difficult it often is for me to honor the basic demands of Christian living. My sense of shame over this incident humbled me. To the extent that humility is involved in Christian spiritual growth, my shame contributed to my spiritual growth.

Understood in this way, we believe that shame can have a *positive* role to play in human life. It can even contribute to spiritual growth, as Karen's experience shows, by holding us accountable for our actions and reminding us that sanctification is a long and difficult road. Shame can serve as a corrective. Shame need not involve a core sense of being unlovable and inferior, but rather a true sense that we have violated an important part of God's purposes for our lives. Thus, we do not think that any action or judgment by a pastor that engenders shame is automatically spiritually abusive. If the parishioner who comes to the pastor to confess an affair feels shame upon leaving the pastor's office, we would not judge that the pastor has been abusive. The presence of shame alone is not sufficient to establish that there has been abuse.

Ironically, we believe that judgment given in love often *does* lead to a sense of shame, precisely because someone may find it hard to believe that the community still offers love in the face of their transgressions. Often people such as Ed come to a pastor precisely because they already feel a sense of shame, or know that they are wrong and are seeking someone to speak out loud what they are afraid to confront openly. A pastor such as the Reverend Stiles might very well begin by asking Ed how he is feeling about being involved in an affair. It will be important for Ed to hear his own unspoken thoughts. The Reverend Stiles probably believes that Ed would not have come to her had he not felt his actions were wrong. An essential aspect of her pastoral task is to encourage him to be the best person he can be. Ed may feel shame, but where shame is a transitory feeling rather than a deeply inculcated sense of personal inadequacy, shame can contribute to spiritual growth. Engendering such feelings is not necessarily abusive.

The Question of Intent

But what if there is not spiritual growth but instead damage done to someone's spirituality? What if the core sense of personal worth or of relationship to God *is* damaged by a pastor's actions? Do all actions that damage someone's spirituality automatically constitute *abuse*, or is it possible that some are simple *mistakes* or are *unfortunate* but not abusive?

Little room is made in the discussion of spiritual abuse thus far to acknowledge that pastors, like all professionals, sometimes make mistakes. Cases in the literature are often extreme examples of power brokering without any limits and seemingly without conscience. But ordinary pastors who are not wielding power in this way may nonetheless harm others.

Are all such harms to be counted as damage that constitutes spiritual abuse? What if there is harm, but it is unintended? Does intent play a role in the assessment that spiritual abuse is happening? We think so. In *Doing and Deserving: Essays in the Theory of Responsibility,* philosopher Joel Feinberg distinguishes three types of "faults":

1. Instances of defective skill or ability;
2. Instances of defective or improper care or effort;
3. Instances of improper intent.[43]

By unpacking these distinctions, we may be able to discern better when it is appropriate to claim that an action or pattern of action that harms someone is "abusive."

Suppose a young pastor, just starting out, is very nervous handling his first funeral. He wants to mix solemnity with a bit of levity, knowing that laughter can have its own healing effects during a time of grief. His attempts at humor, however, are poorly chosen and seem offensive to some members of the congregation. Several complain that he "ruined" the funeral and made it difficult for them to experience God or to be comforted at their time of grief. Using the foregoing distinctions, we would argue that this is an instance of defective skill or ability. The pastor's intentions were good, but his execution of them lacked the finesse that might come with experience. Through his lack of skill, he may indeed have inflicted damage on congregants' spirituality, but we do not think his behavior could be called spiritual abuse. There was no intent to harm anyone; indeed, the goal was precisely the opposite. It was simply lack of experience that led to an unfortunate mistake. There is no spiritual abuse, then, but a defect of skill or ability. We would expect him to regret his actions, but we would not judge them serious failures of professional ethics; rather, they are mistakes, and professional ethics would require simply that he make every effort to learn from them and to improve his skill.

Suppose the same pastor, ten years later, makes the same

kind of mistake. With his years of experience, it is a mistake that we think he should no longer make. He cannot excuse himself by claiming that he is young and inexperienced. In making the same mistake as before, he is exhibiting what Feinberg calls "improper care or effort": he has not tried hard enough to learn what he needs to know. The basic failure is still one of skill or ability, but that failure is now coupled with a different kind of defect: he *should* know better by this time, but has been lazy or negligent in learning what he needs to know. We would probably still consider his mistake to be primarily a failure of skill and hence, not abuse, but we would judge him more harshly, because his behavior appears to involve either a genuine inability to learn a necessary skill for ministry or a character flaw such as lack of effort, not simply a lack of knowledge or ability.

Finally, suppose the same pastor knows full well that his efforts at humor will be offensive but deliberately carries them out, believing that he knows what the people "need" even if they do not agree. If he acts in full knowledge that he will give offense and damage people's spirituality, then we would surely judge him guilty of improper intent. He has broken faith with his parishioners. Now we have moved clearly into a category closer to abuse. Where lack of skill seems to us to constitute a category of mistake or incompetence, improper intent seems to us to move over into a category of abuse.

The significance of these distinctions is readily seen when we consider the plight of feminists seeking spiritual support in mainline denominations. Some pastors neglect to use inclusive language for God because they do not realize that the failure to use inclusive language harms people spiritually. They lack skill and knowledge. Some pastors continue this neglect because they have not bothered to inform themselves of the importance of inclusive language to people's spiritual growth. They are guilty of defective effort. Some pastors know full well that noninclusive language is hurtful to women and men in the church, but have chosen deliberately to use noninclusive language. In our judgment, they are then guilty of spiritual abuse. In short, not every instance of non-inclusive language can be considered abusive, but there are circumstances under which the choice of noninclusive language is indeed abusive.

The same distinctions can be applied to many of the behaviors cited by Johnson and VanVonderen or by the Linns or by others. Rarely does a single act, no matter how offensive or damaging, constitute spiritual abuse.[44] Patterns of action that damage, however, suggest either improper care or improper intent. Improper intent—the intent to abuse, or the self-serving intent to bolster one's position as pastor by belittling members of the church—constitutes unethical and unprofessional conduct, some of which does indeed bring about spiritual abuse. Most of the prototypical cases of spiritual abuse in the literature involve clergy who misuse their power. Even here, however, judgment that abuse is happening is not always easy. For example, if the pastor of a theologically conservative congregation genuinely believes that parishioners must live their lives by rigid rules and must be corrected and brought into line harshly in order to be acceptable servants of God, then that pastor's actions will be harsh and judgmental. Is this an ethically acceptable use of power, or an abuse of power? Enroth, Johnson and VanVonderen, and others clearly think it is abusive. From our perspective, failures of knowledge or skill constitute incompetence on the part of clergy, but are not abusive in themselves, even if they have hurtful consequences. Hence, a theologically conservative pastor who lacks knowledge of a full range of expressions of God's will may hurt others but without any intent to abuse. If there are devastating spiritual consequences from the lack of such knowledge, there is harm indeed, but not necessarily abuse.

Spiritual Abuse of Clergy

Is it only clergy who perpetrate spiritual abuse? If the misuse of power is central to spiritual abuse, then it would seem that only those with the power of the professional role could be the perpetrators of spiritual abuse. Yet many clergy feel that they are not the perpetrators, but the victims of spiritual abuse. While most of the literature on spiritual abuse focuses on abuse of parishioners, Lloyd Rediger's *Clergy Killers* turns the tables. Rediger focuses on the "emotional and spiritual abuse" that pastors receive from their congregations. Since churches as well as clergy are charged with the spiritual care of those in their midst, any discussion of ethics and spiritual care must also look at this side of the coin.

Indeed, there is reason to be concerned. A pastor is forced out of a parish every six minutes in the United States.[45] Moreover, one-fourth of all pastors have been forced out of at least one parish.[46] Nearly half the congregations who fire a pastor have done it before.[47] While Rediger acknowledges that up to 4 percent of clergy may be flatly incompetent,[48] a 25 percent rate of being forced out of a parish suggests that the epidemic of clergy "killing" goes far beyond the expulsions from the pulpit that would be expected on the basis of mere incompetence. Rediger thinks that abuse is going on, and he attributes this abuse to a number of contextual factors, including growing incivility in church and society, distrust of authority in general, theological illiteracy on the part of congregations, and a business mentality that makes congregants see clergy as "hired hands" who can be fired at will. Pastors, suggests Rediger, are no longer "power players" in many communities; they are vulnerable, and not well trained for the trials ahead.

An example of a power play by the laity is offered by Peter Steinke.[49] Twenty-six members of a church sent a letter to a lay leader in a key congregational role arguing that their minister should be asked to resign. First on their list of complaints was "We are not being spiritually fed." Additional complaints included the way the pastor spent his time (too much in community activities and too little in the church), that his style of management was "top-down," and that he was stifling the ministry of the associate pastor. These members of the church were ready to oust their pastor. Was the pastor incompetent? Was he neglecting their spirituality and being spiritually abusive? Or was the congregation being abusive toward a hardworking pastor?

Taking Rediger and Steinke seriously extends our analysis in several ways. First, it reminds us that not all "spiritual abuse" is perpetrated by those with official power or authority. Laypeople who deliberately set out to undermine a pastor can do so, if the church is not vigilant in its spiritual care for pastors as well as for parishioners. Both congregations and denominational officials must bear some responsibility for protecting pastors against vicious attacks or spiritual abuse. Good spiritual care goes in two directions, not just from pastor to parishioner, but from parishioners to pastor as well. A covenant relationship involves both parties, and both are responsible for the spiritual well-being of each other.

Second, Rediger's analysis reminds us that not all conflict constitutes abuse. As we have noted, Rediger distinguishes three types of conflict that happen in the church.[50] "Normal" conflict is the product of diversity and is subject to rational discussion and caring management. "Abnormal conflict" results from a mental illness or personality disorder on the part of one of the participants; rational discussion is not useful in such circumstances, and disciplinary action is needed through "tough love." Finally, there is "spiritual conflict," which happens when one party has become aligned with evil and is bent on destruction of others. Spiritual conflict is a genuine struggle of good against evil, and is not amenable to rational discourse, caring management, or even tough love. In Rediger's view, only "exorcism" or expulsion of the evil is sufficient in these cases. It is helpful to be reminded that conflict alone does not necessarily constitute abuse. Only when it takes on a certain character does it become spiritual abuse.

Nonetheless, we have concerns about Rediger's identification of types of conflict and his application of the typology. First, the boundaries between the types do not always seem clear. For example, Rediger describes one case of "normal conflict" in which a woman minister was finally forced out

149

of the church by a vindictive and determined parishioner. It is not clear whether Rediger intends to suggest that even "normal" conflict can escalate into abuse, or why this case would be called "normal" when another case involving a minister who was almost forced to resign is called "abusive." Is it only the *intent* of the parishioner that makes something abusive? Is it the *effects* of the parishioner's actions? Why is it "normal" conflict when one parishioner begins to talk behind the pastor's back and spread rumors, and "spiritual abuse" when another parishioner does the same thing? We find Rediger's distinction of normal conflict, abnormal conflict, and spiritual conflict helpful to a certain degree, but the distinction among types needs clarification, and it may be difficult in practice to know whether one is dealing with normal conflict, abnormal conflict, or spiritual conflict.

Second, the use of the term "evil" is a bit problematic. We certainly concur with Rediger that evil exists. We further concur that some people align themselves with it. But "evil" is a strong and value-laden term, and we hesitate to apply it. From a Christian perspective, all of us participate in evil to some extent: we are all sinners, or "fallen," even as we are offered redemption. Further, we hold with liberation theologians that much of the evil in the world is structured into systems in which all of us are trapped. Thus, participation in evil may not be a deliberate choice, but a failure to resist the trappings of an evil system. We are sometimes not deliberate perpetrators of evil, but unwitting co-conspirators. An important step toward spiritual growth and health is to bring to light the kinds of tactics evil systems use, and the ways in which systems may entrap everyone.

Nevertheless, Rediger's analysis is salutary in his insistence that clergy can be the victims of spiritual abuse, not simply the perpetrators of it. This suggests either that clergy are not as powerful as is often assumed in discussions of professional ethics, or that power is not central to determining when abuse is happening. We suspect that both possibilities hold.

First, as noted in chapter 2, clergy deal with an *organized* clientele—the church or congregation. There is strength in numbers, and in many church polities, the congregation has power over the pastor. Even in polities where that is not supposed to be the case, denominational officials may find it easier to replace a pastor than to fight with a large and powerful congregation. Thus, being the "professional" in a church setting does not necessarily bring with it the kind of power that would normally be expected in other professional settings. This has been particularly true for women clergy, but is true for other clergy as well. Studies show, for example, that congregational size is an important factor in the dynamics between pastor and congregation. So, we need to be careful not to assume that clergy automatically have power just because they are the identified "professional" in the setting.

Second, although abuse would appear to depend on some exercise of power, people without official power often exercise forms of manipulation that can engender abuse. Crucial information can be withheld from the one in power, so that she makes mistakes that lead to her downfall. Rumors that undermine trust can be spread so that no one trusts the pastor anymore. Trumped-up charges that are ultimately defeated can nonetheless create such havoc in their wake that a pastor is forced to resign. Abuse, in short, does not depend on power alone. Indeed, Steinke suggests that the kind of evil he encounters most often in the church is not overt misuse of power, but is "cunning" and "sly": "subtle manipulation, winsome seductiveness, shrewd innocence."[51]

Further, if a system is itself oppressive or abusive, church members can perpetrate abuse simply by adhering to the system. For example, sexism permeates much of our social order. It defines the way we perceive others and respond to them. Well-intended parishioners who pat the young woman minister on the head are not being deliberately abusive, but they are perpetuating an abusive system that is likely to undermine her confidence, competence, and ability to do her job.

The composite picture of spiritual abuse drawn first in this chapter focused on abuse of parishioners. It suggested that spiritual abuse was linked with abuse of power or perceived power. What we are suggesting here is that the picture is more complicated. Abuse can be perpetrated by those *with* official power and by those *without* official power. Some who have no official power nonetheless have significant unofficial power. They use manipulation and other indirect tactics to control situations every bit as much as powerful clergy sometimes use their power to control situations. Other times, they need not manipulate the system, but simply go along with a system that itself is abusive.

We are also suggesting that when abuse is perpetrated against someone with official power, it need not rely on shame or fit patterns of rigidity or addiction. There need not be an all-consuming system or an overall process that gives one person or group control over another. Although we typically think of abuse as perpetrated by professionals against their clients, there are circumstances in which the tables can be turned. Undermining someone's legitimate authority can be abusive. Abuse here depends not so much on power as on how systems and structures work against truth.

CHAPTER 7

Looking Backward, Living Forward

This has been a "backward" book. In real life, we started with a case of alleged spiritual abuse. This led us on a search for the contours of *good* spiritual care. From those contours, we confronted problems with definitions of both spirituality and "good care." In the book, however, we have presented these in the opposite order, starting with definitional questions and ending with our original concerns about spiritual abuse.

In this process, we confronted a number of significant problems. Two of these we addressed in Part I. The first was sorting through the myriad definitions of "spirituality" that currently dot the landscape. Although we cannot offer a definitive view of spirituality here, we proposed in chapter 1 that those in Christian tradition need to attend to four guideposts as they navigate this muddy terrain. First, a Christian approach to spirituality can utilize broad definitions of human spirit, but must also include an understanding of the divine dimension of life. Second, a Christian approach to

153

spirituality will not rest content with seeing spirituality as something that simply comes easily or flows over one, but will approach and understand spirituality as a dimension of life that requires discipline. Third, Christian spirituality is not simply about individual growth, but requires structures of accountability within a community. Finally, any approach to spirituality that would be adequate must incorporate four dimensions of spirituality: the intrapersonal, the interpersonal, the institutional, and the environmental. Spirituality, in other words, is not simply an "internal" matter or a matter between the individual and God; rather, it encompasses the whole of life and requires attention to matters of structure and to the institutions that so shape our lives today.

The second significant problem was whether traditional definitions of professional ethics are applicable to clergy and helpful for dealing with the question of defining good or bad spiritual care. We noted in chapter 2 that the traditional model focuses heavily on two important features of the professional setting: the power gap between professional and client, and the need for a fiduciary approach in which the professional seeks not his or her own good but the client's good. Cautionary voices have been raised from a number of different directions, however. Some object that this model does not challenge at root the power of professionals; they find inadequate any model that fails to challenge the power professionals have over clients. Others object that women or members of minority groups who are relatively powerless in society in general will not find themselves very powerful in ministry, either. Some argue for friendship or alternative models of ministry that appear to close the power gap. Some suggest that different denominations will have different ecclesiologies, and that these will lead to different emphases for professional ethics for clergy.

Taking all of these challenges into account, we nonetheless conclude that the power of clergy remains morally relevant. Clergy have authority—legitimated power—in several key arenas, such as defining what is happening and assisting people to develop an adequate framework for response. Proper use of this power will be one of the chief concerns in determining whether spiritual care is appropriate or abusive. We also believe that the traditional stress on faithfulness—the fiduciary quality of the professional relationship—applies to clergy, and becomes relevant when we begin to assess whether faulty care constitutes abuse.

With some preliminary guideposts in mind, we turned in Part II to see how we might apply these insights to some typical dilemmas faced by those providing spiritual care. We began our exploration here with clergy who are specially trained to be either pastoral counselors or spiritual directors or both. In the one-on-one setting of spiritual direction, the traditional professional ethics model is helpful. However, in spiritual direction as opposed to pastoral counseling, the interchange between director and directee—or guide and the one guided—is structured in such a way that it avoids some classical problems of transference. Thus, the power differential between director and directee may not loom as large in this setting as it does in classical counseling settings. Although abuse of pastoral power may still be an issue, we think it is less likely to be the central ethical issue of spiritual direction. Instead, we propose that neglect of the four dimensions of spirituality—the "grid"—is a far more serious concern.

When we turn from specialized spiritual direction to the general practice of parish ministry, we begin to see how neglect of the four dimensions looms large. Clergy who interpret spiritual care in terms of individual psychic needs or individual relationships with God may end up neglecting important social dimensions of spiritual care, such as attention to economic issues and stewardship, attention to racism, sexism, or other forms of discrimination that deeply affect spirituality, and so on. Here, we identified a problem that we would not consider spiritual abuse under most circumstances, but that is nonetheless a serious matter for clergy and churches: the problem of spiritual neglect. Some of this neglect derives from a failure to understand the importance of attending to all four dimensions of the "grid." Some undoubtedly derives from a failure to question and challenge the models used for clergy ethics, and to ask what difference it makes to be a professional practicing within a *church* structure, rather than in an individual setting.

Finally, as we look at specialized ministries—chaplaincies, teaching, or secular work that is done as an explicit "called" ministry—we see even more keenly how crucial it is for those doing ministry not to neglect the institutional dimensions of spiritual care. Good spiritual care is not simply about being present or available to those who recognize their spiritual needs and seek help. Often good spiritual care is precisely about restructuring institutions so that they become more life-giving and supportive of people's spirituality.

This review of different settings clarifies several things, in our view. First, good spiritual care will differ from context to context. Second, there are nonetheless some constants in it: good spiritual care attends to more than one dimension of spirituality. In particular, good spiritual care does not neglect institutional and cultural dimensions of life that deeply affect people's spirituality. The lessons of disaffected feminists, and the challenges raised by African Americans and others regarding our neglect of issues of racism, push us to extend an approach to ethical spiritual care far beyond the boundaries of "interior" spiritual work, and to suggest that even "interior" work must be done with a certain kind of integrity that attends to larger dimensions.

With these clarifications in mind, we turned back to our original question: Are some forms of behavior toward another's spirituality so harmful that they should be called "spiritual abuse," and if so, what are those forms? We noted in chapter 6 that Enroth's classic cases of spiritual abuse involved *both* professional power run amok—an echo of violations of traditional professional ethics—*and* institutional failures of checks and balances that left entire systems in place that were abusive. This suggests that spiritual abuse will

156

involve not merely abuse of power, but also institutional forms and failures. We argued that systemic neglect of spiritual needs (for example, neglect of feminist concerns in spirituality) *can* become abusive, where harm is done and the perpetrator has reason to recognize that harm is being done but takes no steps to correct it. We also suggested that a single instance of abuse, such as sexual abuse, can be so damaging to one's spirituality that it can be called spiritual abuse, even though it does not fit Enroth's classic model.

Nonetheless, we raised some questions here as well. We need a way to recognize mistakes or errors of judgment or instances of lack of professional skill in caregiving that may lead to harm, but are not abusive per se. We note that clergy are indeed considered responsible for correcting and directing the spiritual expressions of parishioners, and that this means sometimes that clergy must disapprove of what parishioners do. Not all such disapproval or judgment can be considered "abusive," or we have eviscerated any notion of spiritual leadership. What appears to make the difference is whether correction is given in a spirit of love that intends to lift up and assist the person to get closer to God and to be more fully the person God would have them be.

Finally, we also recognized that clergy deal with an organized clientele, and that the collective power of the laity may be such that they can also abuse clergy. Hence, spiritual mistreatment and abuse is a two-way street. This makes it incumbent upon denominations to put into place structures of accountability not only for clergy but also for churches.

Living Forward

When we began this study, we were concerned that allegations of "spiritual abuse" might begin to float through churches with alarming frequency. In his early study, Enroth focused on certain fringe groups that lacked denominational accountability. His assessment of "abusive" churches was limited to some that had extreme practices and exercised severe control over members. As the term "spiritual abuse" began to gain wider currency, however, it also got dislodged from the specific institutional contexts in which Enroth considered it an appropriate appelation. We heard of at least one insurance company that was indeed threatening to drop its coverage of a large denomination unless that denomination established standards for "spiritual direction" for its clergy. We could envision allegations of "spiritual abuse" being brought to well-meaning clergy who were not feeding their parishioners' specific spiritual needs. We could envision the exponential growth of charges of abuse.

We hope that none of these things will happen. If nothing else, attention to the difference between abuse and neglect, and also to the difference between abuse and incompetence, should result in some caution before allegations of abuse are bandied about the churches. Nonetheless, we also hope that denominations will pay attention to what might become the next wave of allegations against clergy, and that they will be pro-active in assisting clergy to shore up their resources and their skills and in reminding clergy of the fiduciary nature of their work.

This study leaves us with as many questions as it has answered. Parish clergy have ever-expanding workloads at a time when resources are dwindling. People in specialized ministries often do not feel well supported either by the denominations that ordain them or by the more secular settings in which they work. Spiritual directors are working to establish careful guidelines for spiritual direction as this field of professional caregiving expands. In the midst of all this, laypeople in many different church settings often feel that their spirituality has been neglected, belittled, or stifled. We hope this book serves as a call and a challenge: good spiritual care is not easy, and needs constant appeal to the Spirit who sustains us.

In *Deep Is the Hunger,* Howard Thurman says, "There is something incomplete about coming to the end of anything."[1] Certainly this book's exploration of the complex topic of ethics and spiritual care seems incomplete to us. If Thurman is correct, then "one never comes to the end of anything."[2] There is always some remainder, some residue that lingers and "mingles with the stream of one's life forever." Here, we are keenly aware of the residue—the unanswered questions, the struggles that remain for clergy in spiritual direction, in pastoral ministry, and in specialized ministries. At best, we have provided some guidelines and alerted readers to some pitfalls. Accountability structures, attention to all four dimensions of the "grid," recognition of the importance of power and authority, adherence to the fiduciary nature of professional work—all of these we believe are important. But none of them will tell a pastor exactly what to do when confronted with a parishioner whose spiritual growth appears to be accompanied by mental illness. None of them will tell a pastor exactly how to balance the demands of good spiritual care that require attention to economic stewardship with the demands of a dying parish that is afraid to move forward or resists any preaching about sin. We cannot "end" the conversation, but only open the invitation for others to join in asking and analyzing what it takes to provide ethical spiritual care.

NOTES

Introduction

1. Nancy Tatom Ammerman, *Congregation and Community* (New Brunswick, N.J.: Rutgers University Press, 1997).
2. Winifred Gallagher, *Working on God* (New York: Random House, 1999).

1. The Many Faces of Spirituality

1. Martin Marty suggests that this view is increasingly common. Martin E. Marty, "Last Word: Filling a Cultural Vacuum," *Bulletin of the Park Ridge Center* (January-February 1999), p. 15.
2. Rachel Naomi Remen, "On Defining Spirit," *Bulletin of the Park Ridge Center* (January-February 1999), p. 4.
3. John Shea, "Health Care's Transformation," *Bulletin of the Park Ridge Center* (January-February 1999), p. 7. Shea calls this a "popular notion," but it is not his own view.
4. Robert Wuthnow, *The Crisis in the Churches: Spiritual Malaise, Fiscal Woe* (New York: Oxford University Press, 1997), p. 226.
5. Nancy Flam, "The Jewish Way of Healing," *Bulletin of the Park Ridge Center* (January-February 1999), p. 9.
6. Kenneth Leech, *Spirituality and Pastoral Care* (Cambridge, Mass.: Cowley Publications, 1989), p. 5.
7. William Stringfellow, *The Politics of Spirituality* (Philadelphia: Westminster, 1984), p. 19.
8. *Oxford English Dictionary*, Second Edition, vol. 16 (Oxford: Clarendon Press, 1989).
9. Ibid.
10. Bernard McGinn, "The Letter and the Spirit: Spirituality as an Academic Discipline," *Christian Spirituality Bulletin* 1 (Fall 1993): 1, 3-10.
11. Sandra M. Schneiders, "The Study of Christian Spirituality: Contours and Dynamics of a Discipline," *Christian Spirituality Bulletin* 6 (Spring 1998): 1, 3-12.
12. Ronald K. Bullis, *Spirituality in Social Work Practice* (Washington, D.C.: Taylor and Francis, 1997), p. 2.
13. Ibid.
14. Walter H. Principe, "Toward Defining Spirituality," *Sciences Réligieuses* 12 (1983): 135; quoted in McGinn, "The Letter and the Spirit," 5. See also Walter H. Principe, "Broadening the Focus: Context as a Corrective Lens in Reading Historical Works in Spirituality," *Christian Spirituality Bulletin* 2 (Spring 1994): 1, 3-5.
15. Richard Cimino and Don Lattin, *Shopping for Faith: American Religion in the New Millennium* (San Francisco: Jossey-Bass Publishers, 1998), p. 11.
16. Winifred Gallagher, *Working on God* (New York: Random House, 1999), p. xiii.

By "neo-agnostic," Gallagher means a well-educated skeptic who tends to shy away from religion but finds that there is something important in life that eludes the most trusted tools of intellect and learning.

17. E. Glenn Hinson, "Baptist and Quaker Spirituality," in Louis Dupre and Don E. Saliers, eds., *Christian Spirituality: Post-Reformation and Modern* (New York: Crossroad, 1998), pp. 324-38.

18. Theophus H. Smith, "The Spirituality of Afro-American Traditions," in Dupre and Saliers, eds., *Christian Spirituality,* pp. 372-414. Smith proposes that the sociopolitical history of African Americans is fused with the biblical story by means of three aspects of black spirituality: spiritual-transformative dynamics including worship and prayer, spiritual-aesthetic dynamics including music and ritualized speech, and spiritual-political dynamics that represent personal and social history in terms of biblical figures or models (p. 376).

19. McGinn, "The Letter and the Spirit," 1, 3-10.

20. Sandra M. Schneiders, "A Hermeneutical Approach to the Study of Christian Spirituality," *Christian Spirituality Bulletin* 2 (Spring 1994): 11.

21. Miriam Terese Winter, Adair Lummis, Allison Stokes, *Defecting in Place: Women Claiming Responsibility for Their Own Spiritual Lives* (New York: Crossroad, 1994), p. 18.

22. William O. Paulsell, *Taste and See: A Personal Guide to the Spiritual Life* (St. Louis: Chalice Press, 1992), p. 1.

23. Leech, *Spirituality and Pastoral Care,* p. 5.

24. Kenneth Leech, *The Eye of the Storm: Living Spiritually in the Real World* (San Francisco: Harper, 1992), p. 5.

25. Michael Downey, *Understanding Christian Spirituality* (New York: Paulist Press, 1997), p. 49.

26. Ibid., p. 45.

27. Ibid., p. 32.

28. Wade Clark Roof, *A Generation of Seekers* (San Francisco: Harper, 1994), pp. 76-77.

29. Kenneth L. Woodward, "Is God Listening?" *Newsweek,* March 31, 1997.

30. The diversity of groups and agendas is cataloged in Steven S. Sadleir, *The Spiritual Seeker's Guide: The Complete Source for Religions and Spiritual Groups of the World* (Costa Mesa, Calif.: Allwon Publishing Company, 1992). Sadleir lists 17 "spiritual paths," 15 sources for "metaphysical teachings," 31 "masters and movements," and numerous entries on religions.

31. Joseph D. Driskill, *Protestant Spiritual Exercises: Theology, History, and Practice* (Harrisburg, Pa.: Morehouse Publishing, 1999), pp. 43-44.

32. Richard J. Foster and Kathryn A. Yanni, *Celebrating the Disciplines: A Journal Workbook to Accompany Celebration of Discipline* (San Francisco: Harper, 1992), p. xii.

33. Maria Harris, *Proclaim Jubilee! A Spirituality for the Twenty-First Century* (Louisville: Westminster-John Knox Press, 1996), p. 75.

34. John H. Mostyn, Workshop: Certificate in the Art of Spiritual Direction, Supervision Training, Program in Christian Spirituality, San Francisco Theological Seminary, San Anselmo, Calif., March 15-16, 1996.

35. "The Soul At Work," *Los Angeles Times,* April 6, 1998.

2. Ethics for Clergy

1. See, e.g., James F. Keenan and Joseph Kotva, eds., *Can There Be Ethics in Church Leadership?* (Franklin, Wis.: Sheed and Ward, 2000). Stanley Hauerwas should also be credited with giving impetus to the recent rise of interest in virtue ethics among Protestants.

2. See, e.g., Rebecca S. Chopp and Mark Lewis Taylor, eds., *Reconstructing Christian Theology* (Minneapolis: Fortress Press, 1994).

3. See, e.g., Martha C. Nussbaum, "The Discernment of Perception: An Aristotelian Conception of Private and Public Rationality," in *Love's Knowledge: Essays on Philosophy and Literature* (New York: Oxford University Press, 1990).

4. Karen Lebacqz, *Professional Ethics: Power and Paradox* (Nashville: Abingdon Press, 1985).

5. In *The Measure of a Minister* (St. Louis: Bethany Press, 1964), e.g., Dudley Strain declares flatly: "The Christian Ministry has always been a 'profession' and the Christian minister is a 'professional person' in the loftiest meaning of the words" (p. 19).

6. Paul F. Camenisch, "Clergy Ethics and the Professional Model," in James Wind et al., *Clergy Ethics in a Changing Society* (Louisville: Westminster-John Knox Press, 1991).

7. See, e.g., Karen Lebacqz, *Professional Ethics: Power and Paradox* (Nashville: Abingdon Press, 1985). This work drew heavily on Eliot Freidson's *Profession of Medicine: A Study of the Sociology of Applied Knowledge* (New York: Dodd, Mead, and Co., 1973).

8. See, e.g., Edmund Pellegrino et al., eds., *Ethics, Trust, and the Professions: Philosophical and Cultural Aspects* (Washington, D.C.: Georgetown University Press, 1991).

9. Marie M. Fortune, "The Joy of Boundaries," in Katherine Hancock Ragsdale, ed., *Boundary Wars: Intimacy and Distance in Healing Relationships* (Cleveland, Ohio: Pilgrim Press, 1996), p. 86.

10. See, e.g., Urban T. Holmes III, *The Future Shape of Ministry* (New York: Seabury Press, 1971).

11. Camenisch, "Clergy Ethics," p. 131.

12. This argument is made by several authors in Donald B. Kraybill and Phyllis Pellman Good, eds. *Perils of Professionalism: Essays on Christian Faith and Professionalism* (Scottdale, Pa.: Herald Press, 1982).

13. M. L. Brownsberger, "Ethos, Incarnation, and Responsibility," in James P. Wind et al., *Clergy Ethics in a Changing Society* (Louisville: Westminster-John Knox Press, 1991).

14. This is Marie Fortune's catchphrase for the goals of ministry. See Fortune, "The Joy of Boundaries," p. 83.

15. Donna Schaper, *Common Sense About Men and Women in the Ministry* (Washington, D.C.: Alban Institute, 1990), p. 24.

16. H. Richard Niebuhr, *The Purpose of the Church and Its Ministry: Reflection on the Aims of Theological Education* (New York: Harper, 1956).

17. Walter E. Wiest and Elwyn A. Smith, *Ethics in Ministry: A Guide for the Professional* (Minneapolis: Fortress Press, 1990).

18. Ibid., p. 64.

19. Langdon Gilkey, "Forgotten Traditions in the Clergy's Self-Understanding," in Wind et al., *Clergy Ethics in a Changing Society*, pp. 37-53.

20. Rebecca S. Chopp, "Liberating Ministry," in Wind et al., *Clergy Ethics in a Changing Society*, p. 92. A similar comment is made by Gabriel Moran about the professions in general: "At their best, professions continue to be communities of skilled and dedicated people, willing to place an ideal of service above economic self-interest. At their worst, they are islands of privilege for the upper middle class, with a degree from a professional school being the gateway to power and money." See Gabriel Moran, *A Grammar of Responsibility* (New York: Crossroad, 1996), p. 132.

21. Stanley Hauerwas has argued similarly. In *A Community of Character: Toward A Constructive Christian Social Ethic* (Notre Dame, Ind.: University of Notre Dame Press, 1981), Hauerwas, too, suggests that Christian identity is shaped only in and by com-

munity, and that crucial to ethics, therefore, are questions of the virtues that our communities develop.

22. Carol E. Becker, *Leading Women: How Church Women Can Avoid Leadership Traps and Negotiate the Gender Maze* (Nashville: Abingdon Press, 1996).

23. Allison Stokes, "Being a Pastor/Scholar: A Calling Within a Calling," in Berkshire Clergywomen; and Allison Stokes, *Women Pastors* (New York: Crossroad, 1995).

24. Elizabeth Hunting Wheeler, "A New Age Calvinist," in Berkshire Clergywomen, *Women Pastors*.

25. Schaper, *Common Sense*, p. 55.

26. Lynn Rhodes, *Co-Creating: A Feminist Vision of Ministry* (Philadelphia: Westminster, 1987). However, friendship as a model for ministry is problematic for some women. See Rosemary Skinner Keller, ed., *Spirituality and Social Responsibility* (Nashville: Abingdon Press, 1993), p. 306.

27. Mari E. Castellanos, "Barriers Not Withstanding: A Lesbianista Perspective," in Katherine Hancock Ragsdale, ed., *Boundary Wars: Intimacy and Distance in Healing Relationships* (Cleveland: Pilgrim Press, 1996), pp. 197-207.

28. Carter Heyward, *When Boundaries Betray Us: Beyond Illusions of What Is Ethical in Therapy and Life* (San Francisco: HarperSanFrancisco, 1993).

29. Ibid., p. 186.

30. Carter Heyward and Beverly Wildung Harrison, "Boundaries: Protecting the Vulnerable or Perpetrating a Bad Idea," in Ragsdale, ed., *Boundary Wars*, pp. 111-28.

31. Ibid., p. 114.

32. Ibid., p. 115.

33. Ibid., p. 123.

34. Leng Leroy Lim, "Exploring Embodiment," in Ragsdale, ed., *Boundary Wars*, pp. 58-77.

35. Ibid., p. 60.

36. Ibid., p. 73.

37. Lebacqz, *Professional Ethics: Power and Paradox*.

38. See, e.g., William F. May, "Images That Shape the Public Obligations of the Minister," in Wind et al., *Clergy Ethics in a Changing Society*, pp. 54-83.

3. Pastoral Care and Spiritual Direction

1. A. L. Meiburg, "Care of Souls (Cura Animarum)," in Rodney J. Hunter, ed., *Dictionary of Pastoral Care and Counseling* (Nashville: Abingdon Press, 1990).

2. John Patton, "Pastoral Counseling," in *Dictionary of Pastoral Care and Counseling*.

3. Archie Smith, Jr., *Navigating the Deep River* (Cleveland: United Church Press, 1997), p. xix.

4. Joretta L. Marshall, "Pastoral Care with Congregations in Social Stress," in *Pastoral Care and Social Conflict*, Pamela D. Couture and Rodney J. Hunter, eds. (Nashville: Abingdon Press, 1995), p. 171.

5. For an analysis of the shift see Rodney J. Hunter and John Patton, "The Therapeutic Tradition's Theological and Ethical Commitments Viewed Through Its Pedagogical Practices: A Tradition in Transition," in Couture and Hunter, *Pastoral Care and Social Conflict*, pp. 40-42.

6. Howard Clinebell, *Basic Types of Pastoral Counseling: New Resources for Ministering to the Troubled* (Nashville: Abingdon Press, 1966); Howard Clinebell, *Basic Types of Pastoral Care and Counseling: Resources for the Ministry of Healing and Growth* (Nashville: Abingdon Press, 1984).

7. Janet Ruffing, *Uncovering Stories of Faith* (New York: Paulist Press, 1989), p. 13.

8. Ibid., p. 15.

9. Alan Jones, "Spiritual Direction and Pastoral Care," in *Dictionary of Pastoral Care and Counseling.*

10. Gerald May, "Varieties of Spiritual Companionship," *Connections* 7, no. 3 (December 1998): v.

11. Sally Hicks, letter, *Connections* 7, no. 3 (December 1998): v.

12. Patricia Irr, letter to editor, *Connections* (the newsletter of Spiritual Directors International) 8, no. 1 (March 1999): 4.

13. Gerald May, "Varieties of Spiritual Companionship," *Shalem News* 22, no. 1 (Winter 1998).

14. The insights of family systems theory can be useful for understanding congregational dynamics. See, e.g., Edwin Freedman, *From Generation to Generation: Family Process in Church and Synagogue* (New York: Guilford Press, 1985).

15. American Association of Pastoral Counselors Code of Ethics, Principle III— Client Relationships, Section E, Amended April 28, 1994.

16. Ibid., Section G.

17. Spiritual Directors International Guidelines for Ethical Conduct, Adopted by the Coordinating Council of Spiritual Directors International, April 1999.

18. Thomas M. Hedberg, Betsy Caprio, and the staff of the Center for Sacred Psychology, *A Code of Ethics for Spiritual Directors* (Pecos, N.Mex.: Dove Publications, n.d.), p. 8. The Center can be reached at Box 643 Gateway Station, Culver City, CA 90232.

19. *Connections* 7, no. 3 (December 1998): II.

20. See John J. Evoy, *A Psychological Handbook for Spiritual Directors* (Kansas City, Mo.: Sheed and Ward, 1988), pp. 42-48, for some case studies focused on depression.

21. For a discussion of the art and importance of making referrals, see John Patton, *Pastoral Care in Context: An Introduction to Pastoral Care* (Louisville: Westminster-John Knox Press, 1993), pp. 223-26; and W. B. Oglesby, Jr., "Referral," in *Dictionary of Pastoral Care and Counseling.*

22. Hedberg, Caprio et al., *A Code of Ethics*, p. 7.

4. Spiritual Care in Congregations

1. Interview with the Reverend Dr. Sandra Johnson, December 7, 1998.

2. Other issues, such as confidentiality, are equally important, but are already discussed in the literature. See, e.g., Karen Lebacqz, *Professional Ethics: Power and Paradox* (Nashville: Abingdon Press, 1985).

3. It would be interesting to know whether clergy are more reluctant to ask someone to leave when their ill will or attacks target the pastor rather than others in the congregation. See G. Lloyd Rediger's *Clergy Killers: Guidance for Pastors and Congregations Under Attack* (Louisville: Westminster-John Knox Press, 1997) for a discussion of how to deal with negative energy directed against the pastor.

4. The term "excommunication" has a formal meaning in Catholic tradition. It is not used much in Protestant traditions. However, all communions struggle with issues of what it takes to be inside the communion and whether there are grounds for excommunicating members.

5. Rediger, *Clergy Killers*, p. 95.

6. Ibid., p. 60.

7. Ibid., p. 97.

8. Rediger also proposes that we need ethical codes for laity (*Clergy Killers*, p. 143). We concur. Churches should not allow abusive behavior on the part of laity toward other members or toward clergy.

9. For a discussion of evil from a Protestant perspective, we recommend Ted Peters, *Sin: Radical Evil in Soul and Society* (Grand Rapids: Wm. B. Eerdmans, 1994).

10. Joseph D. Driskill, *Protestant Spiritual Exercises: Theology, History, and Practice* (Harrisburg, Pa.: Morehouse Publishing, 1999).

11. We note, e.g., that there are rather careful and extensive guidelines for ethical conduct promulgated in Buddhist tradition. Having respect for this tradition might also imply familiarity with the guidelines expected of practitioners within the tradition. See Alan Senauke, ed., *Safe Harbor: Guidelines, Process and Resources for Ethics and Right Conduct in Buddhist Communities* (Berkeley, Calif.: Buddhist Peace Fellowship, 1969).

12. Personal communication.

13. For Gandhi's views on the equality of all religions, see his "Letter to Narandas Gandhi," in *Gandhi in India in His Own Words*, ed. Martin Green (Hanover, N.H.: University Press of New England, 1987), pp. 134-36; also Jack A. Homer, *The Wit and Wisdom of Gandhi* (Boston: Beacon Press, 1951), p. 16.

14. Correspondence from Gunnar Christiansen, M.D., chair of FaithNet and member of the board of California Alliance for the Mentally Ill.

15. We have noted in chapter 3 that clergy with such clinical training are often members of professional organizations, e.g., the American Association of Pastoral Counselors.

16. Similarly, in *An Anthropologist on Mars*, Oliver Sacks describes an Italian painter whose artistic creativity seemed to go hand in hand with mental aberrations. The painter chose deliberately not to attempt to cure his mental illness, for fear of losing his artistic insight. See "The Landscape of His Dreams," in Oliver Sacks, *An Anthropologist on Mars* (New York: Alfred A. Knopf, 1995), pp. 153-87.

17. Rediger, *Clergy Killers*, p. 85.

18. James Leehan, "Domestic Violence: A Spiritual Epidemic," *The Christian Ministry* (May-June 1992): 15-18.

19. Many states have mandatory reporting laws regarding suspected child abuse. Clergy are bound by these laws. The ethical issues are not resolved, however, by simply adhering to the minimal requirements of the law.

20. Marie Marshall Fortune, *Sexual Violence: The Unmentionable Sin* (New York: Pilgrim Press, 1983).

21. Driskill, *Protestant Spiritual Exercises*, p. 31 (see also p. xiii).

22. C. Kirk Hadaway and David A. Roozen, *Rerouting the Protestant Mainstream* (Nashville: Abingdon Press, 1995), pp. 74-75.

23. Ibid., p. 95, emphasis in original.

24. Ibid., p. 113.

25. C. Jeff Woods, *Congregational Megatrends* (Washington, D.C.: Alban Institute, 1996), pp. 88ff.

26. Ibid., pp. 95-96.

27. Eugene H. Peterson, "Teach Us to Care and Not to Care," in Susan S. Phillips and Patricia Benner, eds., *The Crisis of Care: Affirming and Restoring Caring Practices in the Helping Professions* (Washington, D.C.: Georgetown University Press, 1994), p. 71.

28. Larry Dossey, M.D., *Be Careful What You Pray For . . . You Just Might Get It* (San Francisco: HarperCollins, 1997).

29. Mary Baker Eddy, "Obtrusive Mental Healing," in *Miscellaneous Writings* (Boston: trustees of the Eddy estate under terms of her will, 1986), p. 282.

30. Dossey, *Be Careful What You Pray For*, p. 187.

31. Miriam Therese Winter, Adair Lummis, and Allison Stokes, *Defecting in Place: Women Claiming Responsibility for Their Own Spiritual Lives* (New York: Crossroad, 1994), p. 51.

32. Ibid., p. 45.

33. Ibid.

34. Ibid.

35. Ibid., p. 46.

36. Ibid., p. 122.

37. Ibid., p. 121.

38. Ibid., p. 168.

39. Ibid., p. 37.

40. Ibid., p. 186.

41. Ibid., p. 217.

42. In like manner, Sally B. Purvis identifies Christian feminist spirituality as characterized by inclusive language and practice, a sense of connectedness with all beings and a rejection of patriarchy and hierarchy, a stress on embodiment and the erotic, and an orientation toward liberation (see "Christian Feminist Spirituality," in Louis Dupré and Don E. Saliers, eds., *Christian Spirituality: Post-Reformation and Modern* [New York: Crossroad, 1998], pp. 500-519).

43. Robert Wuthnow, *The Crisis in the Churches: Spiritual Malaise, Fiscal Woe* (New York: Oxford University Press, 1997), p. 57.

44. Ibid., p. 61.

45. Ibid., p. 62.

46. Ibid., p. 148.

47. Ibid., p. 163.

48. Ibid., p. 14. However, giving in "mega-churches" with memberships exceeding 1,000 was considerably higher (see pp. 235-36). The medium-sized church seems to be in the worst position, with members who give proportionately less than either those in larger or smaller churches.

49. Ibid., pp. 120-21, 182.

50. Archie Smith, Jr., *Navigating the Deep River: Spirituality In African-American Families* (Cleveland: United Church Press, 1997), p. 2.

51. See, e.g., George Parsons and Speed B. Leas, *Understanding Your Congregation as a System* (Washington, D.C.: Alban Institute, 1993); Peter L. Steinke, *Healthy Congregations: A Systems Approach* (Washington, D.C.: Alban Institute, 1996); Peter L. Steinke, *How Your Church Family Works: Understanding Congregations as Emotional Systems* (Washington, D.C.: Alban Institute, 1993).

52. Smith, *Navigating the Deep River*, p. 8.

53. Ibid., p. 17.

54. Interview with Sandra Johnson, December 7, 1998.

55. The phrase "interior life" is used by *Booklist* in advertising Diana L. Eck's *Encountering God: A Spiritual Journey from Bozeman to Banaras* (Boston: Beacon Press, 1993).

5. Spiritual Care in Specialized and Workplace Ministries

1. *Los Angeles Times*, "The Soul At Work," April 6, 1998.

2. See William Diehl, *Ministry in Daily Life: A Practical Guide for Congregations* (Bethesda, Md.: Alban Institute, 1996); Lewis Richard, *Work as a Spiritual Practice: A Practical Buddhist Approach to Inner Growth and Satisfaction on the Job* (New York: Broadway Books, 1999); Robert J. Banks, *Faith Goes to Work: Reflections from the Marketplace* (Bethesda, Md.: Alban Institute Publications, 1993).

3. See Alan Briskin, *The Stirring of the Soul in the Workplace* (San Francisco: Berrett-Koehler Publishers, 1998); URL: www.bizspirit.com.

4. See David C. Korten, *When Corporations Rule the World* (San Francisco: Berrett-Koehler Publishers, 1995); Juliet B. Schor, *The Overspent American: Upscaling,*

Downshifting, and the New Consumer (New York: Basic Books, 1998); Richard Sennett, *The Corrosion of Character: The Personal Consequences of Work in the New Capitalism* (New York: W. W. Norton & Co., 1998). Social and theological critique also comes from works committed to justice for the worker or laborer. See Timothy J. Gorringe, *Capital and the Kingdom: Theological Ethics and Economic Order* (Maryknoll, N.Y.: Orbis Books, 1994).

5. Robert Wuthnow, *The Crisis in the Churches: Spiritual Malaise, Fiscal Woe* (New York: Oxford University Press, 1997), p. 6.

6. The facile use of "follow your bliss" as a technique for finding employment makes trivial Joseph Campbell's use of the phrase to note a profound source of human vitality that needs also to be guided by the intellect. *Joseph Campbell: The Power of Myth with Bill Moyers,* ed. Betty Sue Flowers (New York: Doubleday, 1988), pp. 190-93; also *An Open Life: Joseph Campbell in Conversation with Michael Toms,* ed. John M. Maher and Dennie Briggs (Burdett, N.Y.: Larson Publications, 1988), p. 31.

7. Lewis Richard, *Work as a Spiritual Practice: A Practical Buddhist Approach to Inner Growth and Satisfaction on the Job* (New York: Broadway Books, 1999), p. 7.

8. Wuthnow, *Crisis in the Churches,* p. 60.

9. Wuthnow notes that when he was doing his research, one in ten people had been laid off within the past year, one in eight had taken a pay cut, and nearly one in ten had experienced discrimination in the workplace (ibid., p. 61).

10. Ibid., p. 114.

6. Spiritual Abuse

1. Ronald M. Enroth, *Churches That Abuse* (Grand Rapids: Zondervan, 1992), pp. 54-65.

2. Quoted in Miriam Therese Winter, Adair Lummis, and Allison Stokes, *Defecting in Place: Women Claiming Responsibility for Their Own Spiritual Lives* (New York: Crossroad, 1994), p. 21.

3. Quoted in ibid., p. 19.

4. It may also gain urgency, as one case goes to trial: two brothers are accused of several "hate crimes" involving the death of two gay men and the burning of three synagogues in California. Their behavior is being linked to the rigid, demanding, and spiritually abusive practices of the sect to which they belonged (*San Francisco Chronicle,* July 15, 1999, p. 1).

5. G. Lloyd Rediger, *Clergy Killers: Guidance for Pastors and Congregations Under Attack* (Louisville: Westminster-John Knox Press, 1997), p. 2.

6. Archie Smith, Jr., *Navigating the Deep River: Spirituality in African American Families* (Cleveland, Ohio: United Church Press, 1997), p. 38.

7. Michael D. Langone, *Recovery from Cults: Help for Victims of Psychological and Spiritual Abuse* (New York: W. W. Norton & Co., 1993).

8. Flora Wuellner, *Feed My Shepherds: Spiritual Healing and Renewal for Those in Christian Leadership* (Nashville: Upper Room Books, 1998), p. 50; see also p. 46.

9. Matthew Linn, Sheila Fabricant Linn, and Dennis Linn, *Healing Spiritual Abuse and Religious Addiction* (New York: Paulist Press, 1994).

10. David Johnson and Jeff VanVonderen, *The Subtle Power of Spiritual Abuse* (Minneapolis: Bethany House Publishers, 1991).

11. David B. Guralink, ed., *Webster's New World Dictionary of the American Language* (New York: Fawcett Popular Library, 1979), p. 3.

12. See Enroth, *Churches That Abuse,* pp. 31, 72, and passim.

13. "Control-oriented leadership is at the core of all such churches" (Enroth, *Churches That Abuse,* p. 80).

14. Ibid., p. 29.
15. Johnson and VanVonderen, *Subtle Power of Spiritual Abuse,* p. 13.
16. Ibid., p. 20.
17. Ibid., p. 11.
18. Ibid., p. 12.
19. Ibid., p. 22.
20. Ibid., p. 32.
21. Ibid., p. 17.
22. Ibid., pp. 20-21.
23. Ibid., p. 19.
24. Ibid., p. 30.
25. However, it is also possible for clergy to be abused by their congregations, as when a church refuses a minister any vacation or derides the pastor for taking a reasonable vacation (Johnson and VanVonderen, *Subtle Power of Spiritual Abuse,* p. 21).
26. Ibid., p. 30.
27. Ibid., p. 34.
28. Ibid., p. 23.
29. Ibid., chap. 4.
30. For a comprehensive list—"Healthy and Unhealthy Religious and Spiritual Values and Lifestyles"—see P. Scott Richards, John M. Rector, and Alan C. Tjeltveit, "Values, Spirituality, and Psychotherapy," in *Integrating Spirituality into Treatment,* ed. William R. Miller (Washington, D.C.: American Psychological Association, 1999), p. 145.
31. Linn, *Healing Spiritual Abuse,* p. 11. Recall that Flora Wuellner also defined freedom as key to healthy spirituality. See note 8 above.
32. Linn, *Healing Spiritual Abuse,* p. 12.
33. Ibid., p. 43.
34. Ibid., p. 45.
35. Ibid., p. 10.
36. Ibid., p. 15.
37. Michael D. Langone, ed., *Recovery from Cults: Help for Victims of Psychological and Spiritual Abuse* (New York: W. W. Norton & Co., 1993).
38. The Graduate Theological Union Library in Berkeley, California, contains a rather comprehensive collection in the area of new religious groups. See Diane Choquette, *New Religious Movements Research Collection Acquisitions List: 1984–1989* (Berkeley, Calif.: The Collection, Graduate Theological Union Library, 1991).
39. Rediger, *Clergy Killers,* pp. 54-60.
40. Walter E. Wiest and Elwyn A. Smith, *Ethics in Ministry: A Guide for the Professional* (Minneapolis: Fortress Press, 1990), p. 64.
41. Linn, *Healing Spiritual Abuse,* p. 43. Cf. Nancy J. Ramsay, "Sexual Abuse and Shame: The Travail of Recovery," in Maxine Glaz and Jeanne Stevenson Moessner, eds., *Women in Travail and Transition: A New Pastoral Care* (Minneapolis: Fortress Press, 1991), p. 112: "an inner sense of being completely diminished or insufficient as a person."
42. Ramsay, "Sexual Abuse and Shame," p. 114.
43. Joel Feinberg, *Doing and Deserving: Essays in the Theory of Responsibility* (Princeton, N.J.: Princeton University Press, 1970), p. 126. Feinberg calls these "defeasible" faults, meaning that they can be "defeated"—i.e., it is possible to show evidence why they should not be "registered" against us as a fault.
44. There is one important exception here. Inappropriate sexual intimacy between pastor and parishioner is so damaging that a single act does indeed constitute spiritual abuse.
45. Rediger, *Clergy Killers,* p. 6.
46. Ibid., p. 7.

47. Ibid., p. 13.
48. Ibid., p. 105.
49. Peter L. Steinke, *Healthy Congregations: A Systems Approach* (Washington, D.C.: Alban Institute, 1996), p. 51.
50. Rediger, *Clergy Killers,* pp. 54-60.
51. Steinke, *Healthy Congregations,* p. 60.

7. Looking Backward, Living Forward

1. Howard Thurman, *Deep Is the Hunger: Meditations for Apostles of Sensitiveness* (Richmond, Ind.: Friends United Press, 1990), p. 132.
2. Ibid., p. 133.

INDEX